BLOODY MARY

TUDOR TERROR, 1553–1558

PHIL CARRADICE

Pen & Sword
MILITARY

For Dewi and Dad, so many thanks

First published in Great Britain in 2018 by
PEN AND SWORD MILITARY
an imprint of
Pen and Sword Books Ltd
47 Church Street
Barnsley
South Yorkshire S70 2AS

ISBN 978 1 526728 65 4

Typeset by Aura Technology and Software Services, India
Printed and bound by CPI Group (UK) Ltd, Croydon, CR0 4YY

Pen & Sword Books Ltd incorporates the imprints of Pen & Sword
Archaeology, Atlas, Aviation, Battleground, Discovery, Family History, History, Maritime, Military, Naval,
Politics, Railways, Select, Social History, Transport, True Crime, Claymore Press, Frontline Books, Leo
Cooper, Praetorian Press, Remember When, Seaforth Publishing and Wharncliffe.

For a complete list of Pen and Sword titles please contact
Pen and Sword Books Limited
47 Church Street, Barnsley, South Yorkshire, S70 2AS, England
email: enquiries@pen-and-sword.co.uk
website: www.pen-and-sword.co.uk

CONTENTS

NOTE ON FOXE'S BOOK OF MARTYRS

Perhaps the most interesting and informative of reports and records on the burnings that took place during the reign of Queen Mary—Bloody Mary as she is still known—can be found in *Actes and Monumentes* by John Foxe. Better known by the title *Foxe's Book of Martyrs*, the first of four editions published in his lifetime came out in 1561.

By then Mary was long dead and her half-sister was already in the throes of establishing the Elizabethan Settlement, undoing much of what Mary had achieved in her limited but brutal five-year reign. Foxe's book is a combination of woodcuts and reports on the burnings but it is hardly objective. It was, and is, essentially, a work of Protestant propaganda. Coming from the reign of Elizabeth you would probably expect nothing less.

An unashamedly anti-Catholic tract, *Foxe's Book of Martyrs* should be read as such. That does not make it any less fascinating and as a virtually contemporaneous account of the martyrdom of nearly 300 men and women is almost as close as we can get to the events of those five traumatic years.

A shorter, more compact edition of the book was published by Timothy Bright in 1589 and is available to modern readers in facsimile form. The British Academy's Foxe Project, available online, provides an annotated version of the full text and is essential reading for anyone interested in the period.

I make no apologies for using modern English in the quotations I have taken from Foxe. The sixteenth century was a period of transition as far as the English language was concerned and much of the original text is hard to understand for the modern reader. In style and format the language of the time has more in common with Chaucer—'For he was late ycome from his viage/And wente for to doon his pilgrimage': translate that at your leisure—than it does with modern English.

The essential purpose of this book is to provide an enjoyable excursion into the mid-sixteenth century—the emphasis is on enjoyable. Readers who want to experience Foxe's words as originally printed will find the British Academy's annotated version both fascinating and informative—but not necessarily 'enjoyable'.

Foxe, a committed Protestant, escaped martyrdom on the pyres of the Marian persecution by fleeing to the Continent in 1554. After a rootless few months he eventually settled with his family in Basel, Switzerland. Like many ex-patriates of the time he became fascinated by the tales of Mary's martyrs and produced some early stories while the executions were still taking place. Foxe's recordings stretched back into the early days of Christianity with reports and stories about the martyrdom of many of Christ's followers but it is the tales of the sixteenth-century Marian martyrs that really strike a chord with modern readers.

Foxe knew many of the men who were martyred—he had been ordained as a deacon by Bishop Nicholas Ridley, for example, in 1550—and that gave many of his tales a personal touch. He returned to England in 1559, after the death of Mary, and when he considered it safe. The first edition of *Actes and Monuments* came out two years later.

A 1907 depiction of a burning, based on *Foxe's Book of Martyrs.* (Internet Archive Book Images)

INTRODUCTION

Fear is one of the strongest and most persistent of all teenage emotions. Fear of failure, fear of rejection, fear of being different; the list goes on and on. Mary Tudor succeeded to the throne of England on the death her half-brother in July 1553. Mary was no teenage figurehead like Lady Jane Grey who had been briefly installed as an alternative monarch the moment young King Edward died, at least not physically. She was thirty-seven years old, small in stature and some might even say attractive if it were not for the lines of worry and concern across her neck and forehead. And yet there was still something of the undeveloped teenager about this new queen. In many respects she was a repressed adolescent, someone who had never grown up to accept adult values or concepts. Her whole life was dominated by the fears that any normal teenage girl would, sooner or later, have put behind her. This unbalanced personality would probably have survived quite adequately, apart from one thing: she was queen of England, ruler of all she surveyed.

On becoming queen, Mary was suddenly gifted with an unbelievable, almost obscene amount of power. It was power that she was ill-equipped to wield. Rather than create stability and contentment within her realm, she spent her life searching for the love and acceptance she had been denied and in so doing created a web of fear that soon managed to engulf the whole country.

Even the process of Mary's accession was tinged with mistakes and misconceptions. The attempted coup by John Dudley, the Duke of Northumberland who had ruled as Protector during the final stages of Edward's reign, could so easily have succeeded and worked against Mary. However, the plans of Northumberland were quickly overturned, due in no small part to Mary's immediate heroic actions. Northumberland's puppet, Lady Jane Grey—the 'nine day Queen' as she became known—was deposed and Mary ascended to her throne at the head of a jubilant 800-strong procession.

Although there is no denying that she became queen on a wave of popular acclaim it was not just a case of love for her that helped Mary gain her crown. Hatred of Northumberland and all he stood for were equally as important. Unfortunately, that was something Mary, desperate for acceptance and terrified of being rejected, never really understood. Her life up to the moment she became queen—the first woman to be crowned queen regnant of England—had scarcely prepared Mary for such a momentous and awesome role.

Born on 18 February 1516, as a child and adolescent she was by turns revered, rejected, disinherited and finally brought back into the favour of her father, the enigmatic and increasingly psychotic Henry VIII. She lived first in opulence and indulgence, then in genteel isolation and finally in virtual prison conditions where, in fear for her life, she was denied the strong arm of the father figure that she craved and that her fragile personality desperately needed.

With such a dysfunctional upbringing it was hardly surprising that Mary was a flawed and needy individual. She could be dynamic and decisive but, at the same time, she was invariably obstinate and unbending. Often physically unwell,

Mary Tudor, Bloody Mary as she will always be known.

her mental health was equally as fragile. Sadly, after the death of her Lord Chancellor, Bishop Gardiner, in 1555 she did not have advisers who were capable of seeing her problems and willing to offer support when it was most needed. It was to be a fatal absence for her, both as an individual and as a monarch.

The twenty years before Mary's accession had been traumatic. Despite succeeding to the throne in the first peaceful and unchallenged accession for a hundred years, Mary's father, Henry VIII, became increasingly paranoid over the thorny issue of his own successor.[1]

The Tudor claim to the throne was fragile, a case of might rather than right. In the sixteenth century, the need for a male heir was paramount. A queen would probably marry, either for love or as part of an alliance and, by the rules and customs of the time, would become the property of, and subservient to, her husband. If the marriage was to a foreign prince then, for Henry VIII and for many of his subjects, the consequences were too awful to contemplate.

Henry's English Reformation was a pragmatic solution to the secular problem of finding a male heir and continuing the Tudor dynasty. Disposing of his wife, Catherine of Aragon, in favour of the more nubile—and hopefully more fertile—Anne Boleyn was its primary purpose and nothing, not the queen nor the Catholic faith, not the Pope nor the Holy Roman Emperor, was going to be allowed to stand in the way of Henry's desires. Princess Mary was simply collateral damage.

Mary was a devout and practising Catholic all her life, despite pressure to abandon the Mass and accept her father—and then her brother—as Supreme Head of the English Church. Men like Sir Thomas More had already gone to the scaffold for refusing to acknowledge the monarch's position and power but, while accepting the very real risk to her person, Mary was not going to imperil her immortal soul by lightly and easily by making statements which, in her innermost being, she believed to be false.

Even when she was forced, under pain of death, to recognize her father as Supreme Head of the English Church, she did not believe a word of it—and let that fact be known. Empowered by an almost evangelical fervour, Mary held fast to her beliefs, convincing herself that her way was the right way. And when the time came she would prove that to the whole world.

One other aspect, both of adolescent development and of the character of Queen Mary, needs to be acknowledged.

The all-powerful desire for revenge is an emotion that most teenagers experience when things do not go their way, when they are hurt by life or by other people. While it is something that most of them soon grow out of, this was not so with Mary. She could not forget the hurt and humiliation heaped onto the mother that she loved and knew that one day she would seek revenge. Such revenge would not be taken on the king, of course; he would face his own nemesis in front of a greater and more powerful court than Mary's.

But in the mid-1550s men like Archbishop Thomas Cranmer and the bishops Hooper, Latimer and Ridley, who had been pro-active in England's break with Rome and who had been instrumental in the casting away of Catherine and Mary, were still there, still reachable.

As far as these and other leaders in the Protestant establishment were concerned, Mary was a clear adherent to the supposed words of Roman Emperor Nero—'When I am King I shall spare no-one.' If revenge is a dish best taken cold then, by 1553, Mary Tudor had been waiting long enough. It was time to act.

Looking back, with the benefit of much hindsight, Mary's short reign has been blighted by the burnings of the Protestant martyrs. It is almost impossible to study the events of those five years—her foreign policy, her marriage, her relationship with Parliament and so on—without the burnings forcing their way onto centre stage.

Despite her statement on coming to the throne, a conciliatory declaration that she meant 'not to compel or constrain other men's consciences', the hopes of people like

Cranmer and the universal half-belief that Mary intended little more than a restoration of the settlement of her father—effectively a Roman Catholic religion without the influence of the Pope—were soon shattered.[2]

That initial statement of hers was a masterpiece of diplomacy, one that Mary knew was as false as the peddler's quack potions. But for the moment the new queen needed parliament and the men who controlled the intricate government of the state. When she was ready she would show the true side of her character.

The brutality of her reign was intense and earned for her the sobriquet of Bloody Mary. Yet those who lit the fires at Smithfield and other centres of destruction had no doubt that they were in the right. They were doing God's work. That belief applied not only to the men who heaped the faggots and stoked the flames—even while they prayed for the souls of those they were about to destroy—it also fuelled the actions of those behind the burnings, from Cardinal Pole and Edmund Bonner to heresy hunters like the Tyrell brothers and to the queen herself.

The legacy of Mary Tudor remains one of tragedy combined with talent unguided and potential unfulfilled. But overall, it is for her merciless persecution of the Protestant martyrs, gospellers as they were known—men as renowned as Thomas Cranmer or as insignificant as Cardiff fisherman Rawlins White—that she will always be remembered.

They say history belongs to the victor. Like all historical figures, our perception of Mary has been influenced by the work of one of the great 'victors' of the age, someone who survived and escaped the more insane ravages of the burnings. That person was the writer and collector of tales about religious martyrs, John Foxe.

Foxe was dedicated to the celebration of Mary's martyrs and was well able to use literary techniques to emphasize his tales: 'Like any good story teller, he knew the value of a good villain—a role capably filled in this case by Mary Tudor and, farther away, the Pope and the Church of Rome.'[3]

Mary was as much a classical villain as Shakespeare's Macbeth, King Lear—yes, Lear—or Richard III. Like those characters she was not unattractive with many pleasing

Martyrologist and early storyteller John Foxe, the man who more than any other writer or historian helped shape our view of the reign of Mary Tudor.

traits but tragic, doomed and with a fatal flaw or two: ambition, need for acceptance, self-aggrandizement and an inability to separate good advice from bad.

It was as if the part of tragic heroine had been reserved for her and in the end, although Foxe would have been unlikely to see it, a subtle role reversal turned Mary herself into martyrdom as fine as any of the zealots she sought to eliminate.

In her brief five-year reign 284 men and women were consumed by the flames of her 'cleansing' bonfires, a figure that left even the Jesuits and the leaders of the Inquisition in mainland Europe gasping in shock and, if the truth be known, in admiration. Like too many fundamentalist programmes, the Marian persecutions were begun and driven by people with ideals. They were carried out, in the main, by individuals with considerably lower standards about what constituted justice and decent levels of humanity. They were viewed and gloated over by the dregs of society. That was the ultimate tragedy of Mary Tudor.

Where the dynasty started: Henry Tudor victorious at Bosworth Field, by John Cassell (1865).

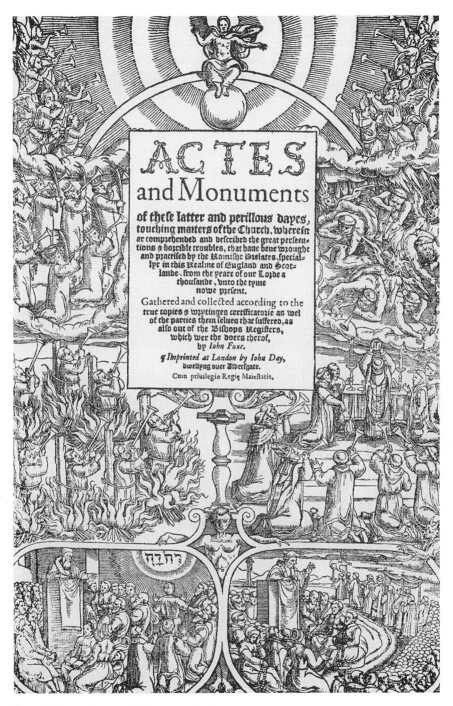

Frontispiece to *Actes and Monuments* by Foxe.

1. A BIRTH IS ANNOUNCED

The king was worried, an emotion that he dealt with in his usual way: snapping at suggestions or trite remarks from his courtiers, hands constantly clenching and unclenching, and rapid pacing back and forth across the stone floors of the palace.

The Placentia Palace on the banks of the Thames at Greenwich was old and more than a little distant from the filth, stench and grime of Whitehall and London. The quickest and most efficient way of getting here—and of getting away—thought Henry, as he paced, was by barge or boat. To ride would take hours, the royal barge half that time.

He smiled and nodded to himself. It had been a good decision of his; there was an agreeably rural atmosphere around the buildings. It was, in fact, the ideal place to bring a child into the world.

Henry himself had been born in the palace, twenty-four years before, and had spent his early months here in rural seclusion. And now he had brought his wife,

Catherine of Aragon, wife of Henry VIII and mother of Queen Mary.

Queen Catherine, to the safe and relatively healthy environment of Greenwich where shortly she would give birth to their first child. Catherine of Aragon had fallen pregnant many times during their marriage but, invariably, the pregnancies had resulted only in miscarriages and still births. This time, Henry and Catherine both knew it would be different. This time there had been no complications and the omens for a healthy delivery seemed good.

He worried—of course he worried—child birth was a difficult time for women whether they were queens or washerwomen. What galled him, however, was that nobody ever seemed to understand that it was a difficult time for men as well. Henry sighed. His routines had already been broken and if there was one thing he did not like it was changing his routines. Still, with the queen now having 'taken her chamber', there would be plenty of opportunity to enjoy life once

Henry as a fit and capable young monarch, from a painting by Hans Holbein.

more, at least for a short period. It would be like being a bachelor again, he decided.

'It is time, sire,' whispered Lord Mountjoy, the queen's chamberlain. 'We must leave.'

Henry nodded and moved to his wife's side. Royal etiquette demanded that the queen should now enter a world of women, a world where men had no place or position. Once Henry and the members of his court left, Catherine would have no male contact until her churching, the purification ceremony that was scheduled to take place thirty days after the birth of her child.

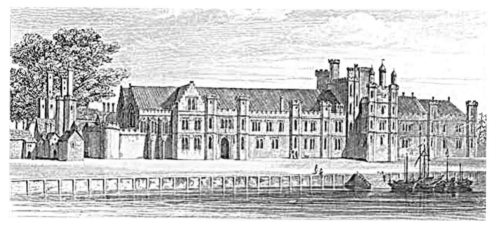

The Placentia Palace at Greenwich, birthplace of both Henry VIII and his daughter Mary.

'I must go, my love,' Henry mouthed.

Catherine smiled at him, weakly, and nodded. Hopefully her gaze would show the king exactly how much she loved him.

'It will be a boy,' she said, taking his hand and laying it on her stomach. 'I can feel it.'

Henry shrugged. 'A boy or a girl, it does not matter. Like you, I hope for a boy but if it is a girl then next time it will be a boy. We are still young enough.'

He glanced to the door, suddenly eager to be away. His head brewmaster had promised him an ale of rare distinction to accompany tonight's dinner. He felt his lips purse and his stomach rumble with the expectation. And tomorrow, whether the queen had given birth or not, there was the wild scramble of the hunt to enjoy.

Henry bent and brushed Catherine's hand with his lips. He felt her tremble and smiled to himself. What it was to have power.

Queen Catherine watched her husband go, his arm draped loosely around the shoulders of some courtier or other. Catherine craned her neck to see who it was but, already, the king was almost out of sight. Henry and his party were moving quickly, as if they had an urgent appointment that could not be missed. 'Poor Henry,' she whispered to herself. 'Life is so simple for you.'

Despite his protestations, Catherine knew that Henry desperately wanted a son. His father had seized the throne after the Battle of Bosworth Field, over thirty years before. He and the Tudors had no real claim so a healthy, strong male heir was crucial to the survival of the dynasty. That simple fact governed all Henry's political thinking.

'God, give me a son,' Catherine said, crossing herself and biting hard at her upper lip.

It was a simple enough rubric for the king, she thought. No male heir, no dynasty—and such a possibility was not to be countenanced. Catherine knew the expectations that were being placed on her; if not this time, she thought, it will have to be a male child next.

'Come, lady,' said one of her attendants, breaking into her reverie and indicating the door to the queen's bedchamber.

Catherine nodded, abstracted, her mind elsewhere. A son, a daughter, did it really matter? It was too late to worry, now. The child, when it finally decided to come—this week, next week, whenever—would be what it was. And she and Henry would love it, of that she was certain. Days of tedium and uncertainty awaited her, despite the opulence of the room beyond the door. Henry? Well, Henry would do what Henry always did best, putting her out of his mind and thinking solely of himself.

'Lead on,' Catherine said and, surrounded by her women, entered the bedchamber.

Some weeks later, at dawn on 16 February 1516, the sleep of Londoners was rudely shattered by the loud and persistent ringing of church bells. Across the city the bells thundered out, from the tiniest parish church to the mighty cathedral of St Paul's. Downriver at Greenwich the queen had given birth to a beautiful, healthy baby girl.

Henry was not unhappy. It may not have been the son he wanted but, as he had told the queen and was later to tell anyone who would listen, he and Catherine were still young and time was the least of their problems. In the meantime, the child was recognized as Henry's heir with full rights to the throne.[1] It was hoped that male children would follow but if not then the arrival of this young princess had at least secured the succession.

As for the baby herself she was christened simply Mary, to be known by everyone as the Princess Mary. Henry doted on her, spoiling her and showing her off to visiting dignitaries at every opportunity.

Mary was a precocious child and with her fair complexion, blue eyes and typically Tudor golden-red hair, she enchanted from the beginning. When she was barely four years old, she

Mary Tudor as a young woman: precocious and attractive, she turned the heads of many influential people in Europe.

entertained visiting French royalty with her performance on the virginals, holding her audience rapt and eager for more. Educated largely by her mother with her strong Spanish views and philosophies, it was inevitable that Mary's religious observations would tend toward the traditional Catholic persuasion. By the age of nine she could read and write in Latin and had a good working knowledge of both French and Spanish. She was beginning to learn Greek and was very interested in music and dance.[2]

The Princess Mary was, potentially, a good catch for any of the monarchs of Europe. Not that anyone ever thought like that. Used as a pawn by her father in the game of 'marriage politics' she found herself betrothed to members of the House of Valois (Francis, king of France) and the mighty Hapsburgs (Charles V) before she had even reached puberty.

Such betrothals were commonplace, part and parcel of treaty obligations and alliances, and could be made and broken with equal ease by either side in the agreement. The age of the betrothed girl was immaterial as no actual marriage could take place until she reached the age of fourteen. As far as her betrothal to Francis, the Dauphin of France, was concerned, he was himself only six months old and would have to wait many years before he could claim his bride, in the unlikely event of the alliance between England and France holding.

Mary's value might lie in the area of treaties and pacts between England and would-be allies but it was helpful that she was pleasing on the eye. According to the Venetian ambassador: 'By this time Mary was developing into a pretty and well-proportioned young lady with a fine complexion.'[3]

Add in her other accomplishments—her musical ability, her flair for languages and her piety—and it was clear that she would be a fine match for any of the great monarchs of Europe. And so it might have gone on, interminably, apart from one thing. Despite his original thinking, for Henry and his queen, time was finally running out.

By 1525 Catherine was forty years old and still the hoped-for male child had not appeared. She had been pregnant twice more since the birth of Mary, suffering the pain of a miscarriage and a stillborn baby daughter. Now it appeared that she was past the child-bearing age.

As if that were not enough, in the mid-1520s Henry had become infatuated by Anne Boleyn of Hever Castle in Kent, one of Catherine's ladies in waiting. He was desperate to court and make love to her but Anne played a brilliant delaying game. She would come to his bed but not as a mistress; her sister had done that and it had led nowhere. She would come only as a wife.

The story of Henry's attempt to have his marriage to Catherine annulled is well known. He found evidence in the scriptures (Leviticus, chapter 20) to support his

Ann Boleyn, mother of Elizabeth. She managed to turn the realm of England and, arguably, all of Europe on their heads.

claim that the marriage had been made against the will of God. According to Leviticus, a man who married his brother's wife would remain childless, a wonderful and convenient explanation for Catherine's inability to provide him with a male heir.

Catherine had indeed been married to Henry's brother Arthur and Papal dispensation had been obtained to allow the subsequent marriage to Henry after his brother's death in 1502. For England the political ramifications of Arthur's death were vast and the recently established alliance with Spain, formalized by the uniting of Catherine and Arthur, was in imminent danger of collapse. Marrying the young widow to the ten-year-old second son of Henry Tudor was an obvious and realistic solution to the problem.[4]

Catherine and Arthur had been little more than children at the time of their marriage. And while Catherine maintained that the affair had never been consummated, Henry now chose to believe that his union with Catherine was against the laws of God. The Pope had been wrong to grant dispensation. To Henry at least the solution was clear: give me an annulment now!

Above left: Prince Arthur, firstborn son of Henry Tudor and the first husband of Catherine of Aragon. His death in 1502 led to political and religious unrest that lasted for over 200 years.

Above right: Henry and his first wife Catherine of Aragon, in gentler and more relaxed times, are shown here at leisure in their garden.

Pope Clement might possibly have granted such a dispensation but Italy had been recently invaded by the forces of the Holy Roman Emperor and he was a virtual prisoner to Charles V, who just happened to be the fond cousin of Queen Catherine. The result was stalemate.

Over the coming months, as envoys shuffled between Rome and London and diplomats like cardinals Wolsey and Campeggio tried desperately to find a solution, the relationship between Henry and Catherine began to break down utterly. Soon the only common thread between the two was their daughter Mary.

Henry, undoubtedly influenced by Anne Boleyn who loathed and felt threatened by both Catherine and her daughter, began to see less and less of Mary. It was painful for both parties but Henry was determined to rid himself of Catherine, bed Anne and provide his dynasty with a male heir. He was soon demanding that Catherine choose between him and their daughter. However badly Henry treated her, Catherine would always be in love with her self-interested and seemingly deranged husband. So there really was only one choice. She would do nothing to further enrage the king with the result that Mary was deprived of the presence and the love of both parents—but in particular her mother—at the most crucial time of her life.

Catherine and Mary saw each other for the last time at Christmas 1530. Cruelly, Catherine was to live another sixteen years, Mary another twenty-eight. And in all that time they had no physical contact whatsoever. Letters passed between them but that was all.

Catherine continued to call herself Henry's only lawful wife and her servants insisted on giving her the title 'Your Majesty;' Henry, never one to be crossed, awarded her the title, Dowager Duchess of Wales but that was more in honour of Arthur, her first husband, than anything else.

The break with Rome became formal with Archbishop of Canterbury Thomas Cranmer announcing, on 23 May 1531, that the marriage of Henry and Catherine was ended. After that the process of Reformation proceeded gradually but inexorably.

The first serious opposition to Henry's religious reforms did not come until 1536 when rebellion and riots broke out in the north of England. The uprising, known as the Pilgrimage of Grace, was ruthlessly put down with the leaders hunted down and hanged. Easily squashed or not, Henry's confidence in his Reformation was

Princess Elizabeth, young and vibrant and, from her earliest days, a shrewd political animal.

The Pilgrimage of Grace was the first major sign—in England at least—of disapproval for Henry's religious reforms. The rebellion was fairly easily put down but the violence and the potential for disaster frightened the king.

somewhat shaken after what had, at first, seemed a relatively quiet and unremarkable disassociation from Rome.

When Anne, now married and installed as the new queen, gave birth to a girl in September 1533 Henry was again disappointed but took Princess Elizabeth to his heart and, as Anne wanted, installed her at the head of the line of succession.

Mary, as the child of the discredited former queen, was deprived of the title princess. She was declared illegitimate and in due course sent to the household of the infant Elizabeth at Hatfield where she was regarded as little better than a servant. Effectively under house arrest, Mary was forbidden to celebrate Mass in public or leave the house without approval. Despite the sudden shock of her changed circumstances, she was determined to be called princess rather than lady as she was now termed and regularly signed herself as such on correspondence. She obstinately refused to acknowledge Anne Boleyn as queen and her father as Supreme Head of the English Church.

Even Thomas Cromwell, the king's powerful secretary and chief minister, was unable to make Mary change her mind. He pleaded and he threatened but to no avail and, eventually, he was forced to abandon the attempt as a lost cause. Neither he nor

Above left: Mary as a young woman.

Above right: Mary Tudor—her reign may have been short but it was one of the most significant periods in British history.

Henry was used to failure and they took Mary's refusal to compromise very badly indeed. Her jewels were taken from her, along with most other personal possessions and keepsakes, and by 1534 she had virtually nothing decent to wear, despite repeated requests to her father for replacement articles. The reply from an Anne-influenced Henry VIII was nearly always the same: when she becomes more subservient.

Mary's response was to keep to her room and shun communal meals in the hall, generally making herself as disagreeable as she possibly could. Her performance infuriated those charged with looking after her but Henry urged them to continue with their work. He did not want his daughter dead, just incommoded and brought up sharp. As Cranmer told him, one day she might just come around. It was a role at which Mary was hugely successful but it was not something that was achieved without immense personal cost. From 1531 onward Mary's health began to deteriorate, partly through stress and partly due to the virtual prison conditions in which she was kept.[5]

An irregular menstrual cycle—something which was to plague her for the rest of her life—and deep depressions, combined with the delayed onset of adolescent emotions, made Mary's life far from easy. All that she had left was her faith, buoyed by regular letters from her mother, now held in Kimbolton Castle.

Ludlow Castle, deep in Marcher territory on the border with Wales. Here both Prince Arthur and the young Princess Mary ruled in grandeur.

Anne Askew, poet and heretic, was one of the victims of Henry's reign, proving that Mary was not the only monarch to burn people at the stake. Tortured, her limbs disjointed, Anne had to be carried to the place of execution and burned while seated in a chair.

A fine example of Tudor architecture, seen here in modern-day Worcester. (Russ Hamer)

It was all a far cry from the heady days of the early 1520s when Mary had been installed at Ludlow Castle with her own household and retinue of servants. She was there to preside over the Council of Wales and the Marches—presumably in title and name only; not even Henry would have been foolhardy enough to entrust such a charge to a tiny nine-year-old girl, no matter how capable and precocious she might be.

During her sojourn at Ludlow, the same place where her mother and Arthur had taken up residence all those years before, Mary had been known as the Princess of Wales. It had been a glamorous and rewarding time, possibly the only time she had felt useful in her short life. Now only continued captivity and possibly even death lay ahead of her. Everything, from her living conditions to her survival, depended on the whim of Anne Boleyn—a strumpet and a loose woman as far as Mary was concerned—and a father who was himself beginning to suffer from illness and the after-effects of a jousting accident which had left him with suppurating and foul-smelling sores on his legs. Mary might be excused for thinking that it was no more than he deserved.

2. THE LADY MARY

The Act of Supremacy, passed in November 1534, made the king the Supreme Head of the Church in England. To deny Henry the right to that title was now a matter of treason and it placed both Mary and Catherine in difficult positions. For a while both of them thought about fleeing the country, if such a course of action was even remotely possible.

Henry kept the coast of England tightly watched and the movements of both Mary and her mother were so well monitored that it would take a miracle for them to get away. They both appealed for help, Catherine to the Pope, Mary to her cousin the Holy Roman Emperor, but nothing came of their requests.

Catherine of Aragon died on 7 January 1536, loving Henry and missing him to the last. She was just fifty years old. Henry, of course, took the opposite viewpoint but by a strange quirk of fate, on the day of Catherine's burial Anne Boleyn gave birth to a stillborn son. It was, many felt, an omen and by spring Henry was already growing tired of his new partner.

The fall and execution of Anne Boleyn later that year, Henry's marriage to Jane Seymour (his third wife) and the birth, finally, of a male heir might have been expected to bring some relief to Mary. It did not. Not to Elizabeth either. Like her half-sister, Anne's daughter was declared illegitimate and was relegated in the line of succession. Henry repeated his demands that both his daughters repudiate the authority of the Pope and accept him as the Supreme Head of the Church. Elizabeth complied but once again Mary refused.

When several of her supporters found themselves in the Tower solely because the king felt they were encouraging her defiant attitude, Mary felt the cut of the executioner's axe on her neck more clearly and more sharply than ever before. She consulted with her close friend Eustace Chapuys, the imperial ambassador, and he responded with advice she might not have wanted to hear but which probably saved her life: '[If] she found evidence that her life was in danger, either by maltreatment or otherwise, then she should consent to her father's wish.'[1]

Chapuys assured her that this was what the emperor wanted and that to save her life, on which the peace and security of all England depended, she must play for time. After all, nobody knew what was likely to happen in the future. A dead martyr would be no use to anyone; a live princess might bring all manner of benefit to the country and to the Catholic faith.

Reluctantly, on Thursday, 22 June 1536, knowing that her declaration was false and that she was betraying everything she believed, Mary gave in. She signed what was known as 'The confession of Lady Mary', acknowledging Henry as the Supreme Head of the Church of England and admitting that the marriage between the king and her mother had been unlawful, even incestuous. She did not believe or accept a word of it. But she signed. Whether she believed it or not, the 'confession' hurt bitterly, and at that moment something hardened inside her. Forced under threat of death to sign a false agreement, she knew that in the future she would never again waver from what she understood to be right. She would go her way.

Henry was deliriously happy that Mary had submitted to his will and had finally acknowledged his leadership of the church. Despite their separation, love for his eldest daughter had not gone away. However, as always with Henry it was love on his terms but it was, at least, affection of a sort.

Mary was immediately restored to Henry's favour and clad now in clothes and jewellery she had thought never to see again, was re-admitted to the court. For the first time in five years she spent a Christmas with the royal family where she was joyously accepted by Henry and his new queen, Jane Seymour. Jane had a genuine affection for Mary and the two women quickly formed a strong bond that lasted until Jane's life was cruelly cut short the following year.

When Jane died just twelve days after giving birth to Henry's longed-for son, Mary was the chief mourner at her funeral. Henry was devastated at the loss of his wife but his one consolation lay in the fact that he now

Jane Seymour, Henry's third wife and mother to the longed-for male heir.

Edward VI was destined for a short reign but when he succeeded his father in 1547 he was fit and healthy, the very essence of a Renaissance prince.

had the son he had so earnestly hoped for over the years. Prince Edward was fit and healthy and with no fears for his safety, it seemed as if the king's tactics had worked.

From left: Philip II of Spain, Queen Mary, Henry VIII, Edward VI and Elizabeth I—an allegorical depiction of Henry's family.

Despite the break with Rome, Henry had always been a moderate, even conservative, in his religious views and policies. He was certainly no Lutheran and his only argument with the Church of Rome was a pragmatic one—it had failed to grant him an annulment when he had wanted it. His views had not stopped Henry from making a fortune by selling off church and monastic lands in what was a typical set of double standards but as far as faith and doctrine were concerned Henry remained a traditionalist. In 1539 the Act of Six Articles was passed by parliament, legislation that confirmed the Catholic nature of the English church—albeit without the leadership of the Pope.

The Six Articles reaffirmed issues like the doctrine of transubstantiation, the celibacy of the clergy and the validity of private Mass, all of which were part of the Catholic service: 'The English church was now definitely committed to an orthodox position, and anyone denying these articles was to be burnt as a heretic.'[2]

King Henry died on 28 January 1547.

Grossly overweight and unable to do much more than sit around trying to breathe, he was a far cry from the robust athletic champion whose appearance and strength had once held all of Europe in awe. The sores on his legs gave off a rancorous odour, making a mockery of his comment about his fourth wife Anne of Cleaves: that she stank, Henry said. If anybody in that relationship smelled badly it was certainly not Anne.

Edward, the son and heir Henry had striven so hard and so brutally to obtain, was still a minor, just nine years old. It meant that until he came of age the day to day government of the country would be vested in the hands of a protectorate of influential and experienced nobles.

The final years of Henry's reign had been turbulent. Three new queens— Anne of Cleaves, Catherine Howard and Catherine Parr—war with France and the execution of Thomas Cromwell had all rocked English society. For Mary the increasingly anti-Catholic nature of

Henry as an old and prematurely aged man. His final years were painful as ill-health and paranoia began to seep into his mind and body.

her brother meant that she must have viewed the coming reign of Edward VI with more than a slight degree of trepidation.

For most of the English population it was rather different. He might be under age but the accession of Edward VI, a healthy , handsome and fit young man who hopefully had many years ahead of him would, it was confidently believed, bring stability and further prosperity to the country.

The members of the protectorate led initially by the Duke of Somerset and then by the Duke of Northumberland, were strongly Protestant in their religious convictions, as was the new monarch. The two lord protectors in particular saw Edward's minority as a chance to develop and firmly establish the Protestant church in the minds and daily life of the English people.

Six months after Henry's death radical new injunctions were issued. These included authorization to destroy images in churches, a prohibition on the use of rosary beads and of candles on altars. There were also strict limitations on the use of church bells.

More importantly, priests were instructed to preach regularly and to read in English rather than Latin, the Lord's Prayer and other significant articles as part of the Sunday service. Within three months, it was ordered, every parish in the land was to own an English version of the Bible which although expensive was now readily available.

Mary watched these and other assaults on her religion and saw no other course of action but to stick firmly to her faith. She had signed her confession and, for the moment at least, was relatively safe. Yet everyone knew of her allegiance to Rome and despite the hoped-for stability of a new monarch and a new regime, it was still early days. It would not take much for her to come face to face with real danger once more.

The 1549 Act of Uniformity made Thomas Cranmer's *Book of Common Prayer* the most significant publication since the Bible. It gave clear guidelines for the way services were to be held and was the only acceptable form of worship in England. By the terms of the Act there was also to be a reduction in the number of Saints Days and the Mass was to be said in English. Mary, still continuing to hear as many as four masses every day—in Latin—kept well away from court, preferring to remain on her estate at Kenninghall in East Anglia where she could worship more or less as she pleased.

There was undoubtedly a strong bond of love between her and Edward but their religious differences were pushing them further and further apart. Both were intransigent, both were committed to their faith and there seemed, even at that early stage, no way out of the dilemma. Agreeing to come to London for the Christmas celebrations of 1550, Mary had immediate cause to regret her decision. She was subjected to public humiliation when Edward rebuked her in front of the whole court for failing to conform to his laws on worship.

A simple comment escalated into a full-blown debate that ended with both Mary and Edward in tears. Edward, still a young boy, was soon able to move on from the argument; Mary, with her repressed adolescent fears and feelings of inadequacy, was not and she left court once the Christmas celebrations were over vowing never to subject herself to such an experience again.

When it was reported that Mary continued to hear Mass in Latin, complete with incense burning and bells pealing, she was informed that she would no longer be allowed to celebrate Mass in her house. Naturally she refused and, in due course, Chancellor Sir Richard Rich and William Petre, first secretary, were sent to challenge her and force her to comply with the new legislation. Mary had gone toe to toe with Henry VIII and Thomas Cromwell; lightweights like Rich and Petre were not going to influence her. She refused and continued to celebrate Mass in Latin.[3]

In 1550 in rural areas such as Cornwall and Devon there were rebellions and riots against the introduction of the *Book of Common Prayer*. They were not so much uprisings against the king or the theological content of Cranmer's book as expressions of concern about losing an old and comfortable friend. Most of the congregation could not understand the Latin of the old service but at least it was familiar and safe. Further disturbances in Suffolk and Hertfordshire were caused by the policy of enclosure of common land and in Norfolk Robert Kett led a rebellion that happened to coincide with war against France. Mary, who owned several estates in the East Anglia area, came under suspicion of being involved. Denying any involvement, Mary clung to her beliefs but, increasingly, her situation was both difficult and dangerous.

Driven almost to despair by the intransigence of his sister, Edward threated Mary with a process of forcible instruction into the Protestant faith. Unfortunately for him, as long as war with France was either raging or being threatened, England needed the support of Charles V and the Holy Roman Empire and thus Mary's

Sir Richard Rich, Chancellor of England, a man best known for his betrayal of Thomas More and his hands-on torturing of Anne Askew in the Tower of London.

London streets in the Tudor period.

position was safe. If and when peace came she knew that she would again find herself in very real danger.

Plans were laid for her to escape the country. In the summer of 1550 Charles sent three warships of the Imperial Fleet to cruise off the Essex coast, ready to lift her to safety. Apart from the dangers inherent in any form of flight, Mary was acutely conscious that she needed to be in England if there was to be any hope of her succeeding to the throne. She decided to remain where she was and the plan was shelved.

Throughout 1551 pressure on Mary continued. That Easter Edward summoned her to court once more and reluctantly—remembering the shame of her previous Christmas visit—she came, attended by upward of 400 retainers and ladies-in-waiting, all carrying rosary beads in a powerful and symbolic gesture of defiance.

The Easter discussions between the two siblings ended in stalemate. Neither would back down and Mary finally declared that Edward was too young to make important decisions about matters on religious belief and tolerance.

The Emperor, Charles V, now entered the fray in earnest. On 19 March he threatened to declare war against England if his cousin was not allowed the right to worship as she wished. As Holy Roman Emperor, Charles could call on large numbers of ships and troops—if nothing else he could starve England into submission.

The Tower of London, the final resting place of many rebels, heretics and, it must be admitted, of innocent men and women.

Faced by the prospect of conflict, the government became inclined to turn a blind eye to Mary's religious practices, very much as had been the case previously. Archbishop Cranmer, always the most virulent of Mary's opponents, urged the king to take action—to knowingly allow sin was, he declared, a sin in itself. And so the debate raged on.

It wasn't all aggression and unpleasantness. The young Jane Dormer, who entered Mary's household at Kenninghall as an attendant, recorded that it was a prestigious appointment: 'In those days the house of this Princess was the only harbour for honourable young gentlewomen, given any way to piety and devotion ... the greatest lords in the kingdom were suitors to her to receive their daughters in her service.'[4] Jane, whose main duty was to read to Mary, would have had little knowledge or understanding of the political pressures on the princess. Respite was, however, waiting in the wings.

By the end of the traditional Christmas and New Year festivities, in 1553 it was obvious to everyone that Edward was no longer the young, fit boy who at his succession to the throne had promised so much. By now he was seriously ill and doctors could do nothing to halt the decline. His body had become wasted and he was constantly coughing up phlegm. It looked like a clear case of tuberculosis and for that there was no cure. It was just a matter of time.

For Mary it meant that there were to be no more attempts to force her into compliance as she might, within a relatively short period of time, become queen. And as the time-servers at court knew only too well, it was best not to make too big an enemy of an incoming monarch.

Edward's decline continued and by the summer of 1553 he was near the end. His sputum was now black, his feet were swollen and he was running a constant fever.

By the terms of Henry's will Mary was her brother's rightful successor but the protector Northumberland and Edward himself both viewed that prospect with horror. Mary, they knew, would restore Catholicism and destroy all the work of the previous decade. They had to act—and they had to act quickly.

That summer Edward drew up 'My Device for the Succession', a document that he wrote and penned for himself although the hand of the Duke of Northumberland, self-serving as ever, was clearly present in its origins. In Edward's weakened state it must have been done at immense physical and emotional cost to the young man and it was revolutionary in its contents.

According to the 'Device', both Mary and Elizabeth were excluded from inheriting the crown because of their illegitimacy. The succession was transferred to the Grey family, the descendants of Henry VIII's sister Mary and therefore Edward's cousins. Despite Edward's belief that women were unfit to wear the crown there were no males in the family and that left Lady Jane Grey as first in line for the throne, at least until she gave birth to a son.

My deuise for the succession.

For lakke of issue of my body. To the L Frances heires masles, To the L Janes heires masles, To the L Katerins heires masles, To the L Maries heires masles, To the heires masles of the daughters which she shal haue hereafter. Then to the L Marg gets heires masles. For lakke of such issue, To theires masles of the L Janes daughters To theires masles of the Kateruns daughters and so furth til you come to the L mar gets heires masles.

Edward's hand-written 'Device for the Succession'.

England's coat of arms, 1554–58, being England's previous coat of arms blended with that of Spain's. (Ipankonin)

Northumberland's plan now rolled into operation. He had quickly married Lady Jane Grey to his son Guildford Dudley—not something Jane viewed with any great pleasure—with the intention of preventing her, as queen, from marrying any foreign prince or monarch. The marriage was also arranged in the hope that Lady Jane would soon conceive a male child to ensure the succession and keep Northumberland in a position of power.

Early in July Mary was summoned to the bedside of her dying brother. Her natural instinct was to go until she realized that it was a trap. Northumberland simply wanted to make a prisoner of her, to put her out of the way while his puppet-queen assumed power.

After that, she knew, it would be a quick knife in the ribs. Mary fled into the night. Accompanied by just six attendants, she began a dramatic ride through darkened countryside that finished at her residence, Kenninghall in Norfolk, on 7 July. It was here that Mary learned Edward had died the previous day.

Edward's passing was received with mixed emotions by the people of England. Those who had kept to the Catholic faith welcomed the news as it meant that a Catholic monarch would soon be sitting on the throne of England once again. There were many for whom the 'old faith' with its familiar chants and rituals, its holy relics and its obvious love of pageant, held a considerable appeal.

Edward, who thanks to the controls of Somerset and Northumberland, had had little dealing with the general public but he was still eulogized in the usual fashion: 'Tenderly beloved by all his subjects, but especially the good and learned sort, and yet not so much beloved as also admired by reason of virtue and learning which in him appeared above the capacity of his years.'[5]

Eulogies apart, the Duke of Northumberland had little time and inclination to mourn the dead king. Lady Jane Grey was proclaimed queen on 19 July, the same day that the Privy Council received a letter from Mary, ordering them to make the announcement that she was Edward's successor and the rightful monarch. From then on events moved quickly. Northumberland had been surprised by the lack of popular acclaim for Lady Jane Grey. Nevertheless, his forces—including artillery and a number of warships on the Thames—soon took control of the city of London, making him secure enough to leave the metropolis behind in order to deal with what he perceived as a far greater problem. On 14 July, accompanied by 6,000 soldiers and field guns, he set out for Norfolk to apprehend Mary.

With typical Tudor energy and resolve, Mary had assembled an army at Kenninghall but soon, marched it farther south and closer to London. She came to rest at another of her properties, Framlingham Castle in Suffolk. She arrived, unveiling her standard on the gate house of the castle on the evening of 12 July and there she waited.

As time went on it became clear that popular support, in East Anglia at least, lay in favour of Mary. The crews of five ships in Orwell harbour, previously belonging to King Edward, mutinied and went over to Mary's side. Her army was swelled by the constant arrival of more soldiers and supporters. Many were ordinary farmworkers, peasants, but they were willing and there was a sufficient number of experienced troops to marshall them into line.

By 15 July, Northumberland and his forces had reached Bury St Edmunds, just twenty miles from Framlingham. Mary, supported by numerous country gentlemen and knights like Lord Wentworth, had by now managed to turn her motley collection of untrained supporters into a well-drilled, competent army.

Framlingham Castle where Mary raised her standard in the autumn of 1553.

When she reviewed her troops Mary was received ecstatically and, with a clear understanding of the common touch, she dismounted and spent several hours carrying out the review on foot. Everyone, from Mary and her commanders to the lowliest drummer boy and footman, looked forward to the coming battle. It never happened, mainly because the privy councillors back in London could not forget that Mary, when all was said and done, was the daughter of the much-loved Henry VIII. They began to waver, to change sides, and with Northumberland not present to bully them into submission, most realized that support for Lady Jane Grey was leading them down a blind alley. The Privy Council soon issued a proclamation offering a reward of £1,000 to any nobleman or £500 to any yeoman who managed to capture Northumberland, for whom it was the beginning of the end.

To widespread rejoicing, Lady Jane Grey was deposed and, along with her husband Guildford Dudley, incarcerated in the Tower. On 20 July Mary, amidst great rejoicing in the streets of London, was proclaimed queen. Resting now at Cambridge, the Duke of Northumberland could do nothing more than admit defeat. He apparently threw his hat into the air and shouted, 'God bless Queen Mary' in a cringeworthy attempt to crawl into Mary's favour. Mary showed her disdain: within hours Northumberland was arrested for treason—in the name of Queen Mary.

Right: John Dudley, Duke of Northumberland.

Below: England saw no shortage of armed fighting men in the Tudor period, particularly farther north. Shown here in a re-enactment are what were known as Reivers, armed bandits who raided across the Scottish border region. (Malcolm Carruthers)

3. QUEEN AT LAST

Mary made a triumphant entry into her capital on the evening of 3 August 1553. She was accompanied by her half-sister Elizabeth and a procession of over 800 men and women. According to some reports, a crowd of over 10,000 people thronged the streets to welcome her. Always fastidious about her appearance Mary took pains to ensure that she made an impression on her subjects and was well dressed for the occasion. She wore a splendid gown of velvet over a kirtle of purple satin with a large, striking headdress. Pearls sewn into the edging of her gown and a gold necklace completed her outfit.[1]

Fine clothes could not disguise the obvious effects of worry and ill-health, however, and Mary looked prematurely old. By contrast, the twenty-year-old Elizabeth appeared to be in the full bloom of life. It was a comparison that the public could not help making.[2]

One of Mary's first actions as queen was to order the freeing of Bishop Stephen Gardiner, a long-time opponent of the Reformation and an ardent Catholic. It was an important and sensible decision, one she never had cause to regret.

Mary as queen of England and Ireland.

On his release from the Tower of London, Mary had a personal interview with Gardiner who was quickly appointed to the Queen's Council. He was happy to be involved, particularly when he was also made Bishop of Winchester. Three weeks into Mary's reign he became Lord Chancellor.

A generous and humane man, Gardiner had made a name for himself in the reign of Henry VIII, working for Cardinal Wolsey and for the king himself, but his opposition to the Reformation—from a doctrinal point of view—later saw him condemned to Fleet Prison and then to the gruesome reality of the Tower. By the time of his release Gardiner was an old man with only a few years to live but he still had the energy to support and advise the queen. How much influence Gardiner had on Mary's policies remains unclear, particularly as her first port of call for advice was usually her cousin Charles V. Even so Gardiner was certainly a capable man, an expert in canon and civil law.

They quarrelled once, over the issue of a suitable husband for the queen but it was a short-lived spat and Gardiner, knowing his place, begged her pardon. When he died in 1555 Mary lost probably the most astute and objective of all her advisers.

To begin with Mary adopted a policy of appeasement, rather like her grandfather Henry VII who tended to keep opponents alive but imprisoned in case they might be of use at some

Bishop Stephen Gardiner, the most capable and loyal of all Mary's advisers. On her accession to the throne in 1553, he was released from imprisonment in the Tower and was soon Lord Chancellor of England.

later stage. She looked carefully at the men who had challenged her right to succeed and decided to follow her grandfather's policies.

Many of what Mary called her rebels were allowed to live, albeit on very long and tenuous leads. Even Lady Jane Grey and her husband Guildford Dudley, though convicted of treason, were spared the axe and detained in prison. The fate of the Duke of Northumberland was a different matter and Mary was quick to heap the coals of justice upon his head. Despite his attempts to curry favour, within two weeks of her accession he was accused, tried and found guilty of treason, going to his death at the end of August. The London mob and the people of Norfolk—he had dealt very harshly with the followers of Kett's rebellion in that county—would have expected nothing less.

Within days of Mary's accession, Edward VI was buried in Westminster Abbey. It was a Protestant service conducted by Archbishop Cranmer who, in these early days of the reign, seemed to have escaped destruction. Mary did not attend either the funeral service or the burial.

During the first few months of her reign, altars and crucifixes, statues and reliquaries, quickly began to re-appear in churches across the land and once again

The Palace of Whitehall, principal royal residence during the Tudor period.

Latin was heard in the early Mass and at Sunday services. However, re-establishing the Catholic Church was never going to be an easy process and the physical manifestations of the old religion were particularly difficult to rebuild or recreate: 'The material situation that Mary's church inherited was dire. In five years Edward's regime had bulldozed away centuries of devotional elaboration, and had stripped bare the cathedrals and parish churches of England.'[3] As part of Henry's and Edward's Reformation, dozens of statues, paintings and stained-glass windows—anything in any way connected with or tainted by idolatry—had been mercilessly destroyed. Almost all of the country's altars had been pulled down and broken up; many had been cannibalized for use as pavement slabs, walls or roadways. Those statues and wall paintings that had been left in place had been deliberately vandalized, the faces of statues blanked out with whitewash and paint or had noses and ears smashed.

It was not just architecture. Books and manuscripts of sacred hymns and psalms had been scattered to the four winds, many of them burned, and they were irreplaceable. It resulted in the rich vein of religious choral singing and poetry that had once played such a dominant part of the church service being lost to generations of English worshippers.[4]

As Edward's Reformation had gathered pace, vestments and crucifixes had been simply taken out of the churches and thrown onto the flames of billowing bonfires. Anything that was liable to bring in money—rich cloths, jewels, silks and other luxury items—were ruthlessly harvested and sold. Much of the money raised had gone to the country's war chest, paying for military campaigns across Europe. Replacing them would take time and effort.

Money, naturally, was an issue. It would cost a small fortune to replace the altars and paraphernalia, the shrines and the relics that had been destroyed. It is a tribute to Mary's control of finances and the effectiveness of her Treasury officers that re-establishing the previous physical grandeur of the Catholic Church did not bankrupt the country.

Then, of course, there were the monastic and abbey lands that had been sold off after 1536. These, initially going to the crown, were too valuable an asset for Henry to waste and had been sold on. Most were now resting easily in private hands. And many of the owners were either the great landlords of the country or the nouveau riche. Neither group was going to let them go easily.

Despite the problems, Mary and the senior members of her church, men like Gardiner and Cardinal Pole—the latter sent to England as papal legate in order to help re-establish the Catholic Church—were committed to the job of rebuilding the physical manifestations of their religion. It was, after all, a recognized and expected part of the Catholic tradition.

Cardinal Reginald Pole came from a wealthy and influential English family and was violently opposed to Henry's Reformation. He had left England for Italy in 1532 and when Henry wrote to ask him for his opinion about the dissolution of the monasteries and the break with Rome Pole responded by sending him a copy of his pamphlet 'In Defence of the Unity of the Church'.

The booklet demanded that Henry repent for his recent actions, in particular for the break from Rome. The king, naturally enough, was furious, demanding that Pole should be extradited as a traitor. He also took terrible revenge, knowing he could not get at the future cardinal but could attack his family. He imprisoned and executed most of Pole's remaining

Cardinal Reginald Pole who, along with Bishop Gardiner, helped design and guide Mary's counter-reformation. After Gardiner's death in 1555 he was, briefly, the most powerful man in the country.

family members on trumped-up charges of treason. The execution of his mother Margaret was a particularly brutal affair.

Margaret Pole, the Countess of Salisbury, was Mary's godmother. She had been instrumental in bringing up the young princess and Mary often referred to her as 'my second mother'. Without even the luxury of a trial, the sixty-eight-year-old countess was imprisoned and on 27 May 1541 went to the block. The inexperienced axeman botched the job and literally hacked her to pieces.

Pole was a man of great ambition. He had, at one stage, harboured an idea that he might like to marry Mary and had even come within a few votes of being elected pope after the death of Clement. Always intended for a return to England, he was appointed cardinal by Pope Julius III in the wake of the Pilgrimage of Grace in 1536 when 40,000 men had risen, demanding a return to the old faith and a restoration of the monasteries.

By the time Pole was ready to return to his native land—a desperately dangerous task if it had come off—the rebellion had been put down and there was no purpose in him putting his life at risk. A return was certainly far safer once Mary became queen and, after receiving the official invitation, he finally arrived back in England in November 1554.

Thomas Cranmer had been in prison for several weeks when, on 13 November 1555, he was deprived of the see of Canterbury. Cardinal Pole—who had now taken holy orders—was appointed Archbishop of Canterbury in his place. Like Bishop Gardiner, Pole was at the forefront of the re-creation of the Catholic Church in England and certainly would have an active role to play in the burnings yet to come.

Mary's coronation took place on 1 October when she was crowned as both monarch and, by an irony that cannot have been lost on her, Supreme Head of the Church. She would need to be more secure before handing that particular chalice back to the Pope. The ceremony was a full Catholic Mass where Mary, accompanied by Elizabeth and her former stepmother Anne of Cleaves, was anointed with oils specially sent by Charles V from his provinces in the Low Countries.

The coronation was a vitally important start to Mary's reign, more important perhaps than that of any male monarch as it laid out exactly how she intended her reign to proceed. At the coronation she accepted the full regalia of a male monarch and the sacral role that had previously been given solely to kings: 'Previously, it had been precisely the exercise of this semi-priestly power, derived from the coronation that, it was argued, precluded women from acceding to the throne. By continuing practices undertaken by previous Kings—providing the healing touch for the "king's evil" [scrofula] and blessing rings believed to cure cramp and epilepsy—Mary showed that the office of a crowned monarch was not at all limited by gender.'[5]

Mary had to proceed cautiously. She opened her first parliament a few days after her coronation, conscious that many members of the Commons were afraid they would lose the monastic lands they had bought from the crown after the Dissolution of the Monasteries. It stood to reason that the members would not countenance any loss of property; before a full return to Rome could be considered there would need to be some form of trade off or protection of their recently acquired wealth.

While there had been no precedent for crowning a queen regnant, there was a first time for everything and Mary was prepared to fit in with arrangements. Just as important, however, she was conscious of her lineage. Everyone knew that it was only the Tudor monarchy that stood between peace and a renewal of civil strife in the country: 'Though no woman had sat upon the English throne since Matilda (who had, incidentally, never been crowned) it was sufficient for Mary and, subsequently, for her sister Elizabeth, that they were children of a Tudor King.'[6]

That Tudor lineage was vitally important. Mary might deplore it and wish for a return to life as it was before her father's Reformation, with her subjects accepting yet another change of direction purely on the basis of faith and tradition but she had to be realistic.

She had to accept that this was something she would have to endure, at least until she was more secure on her throne. There were already rumblings of disquiet in some quarters and to move too quickly, Pole told her, might well bring about open revolt. Nevertheless, a slow and steady process of counter-reform began.

Mary and Elizabeth had not always been close. If there had been any particularly strong filial bond it had been between Mary and Edward, not the two sisters. But Elizabeth was already a shrewd politician and knew how to play the game. She would do nothing to put herself at risk.

At one stage she even asked Mary for books to help her understand the Catholic religion and she at least made a show of compliance by attending Mass. The moment Mary was not looking, however, Elizabeth's attendances quickly fell away. The new imperial ambassador Simon Renard warned Mary not to trust her half-sister. Elizabeth was not above throwing herself to the ground and wailing pitifully, asking for help or support: she was, as she always would be, the consummate actor. Mary was not fooled but as long as Elizabeth did not cause too much trouble she was prepared to tolerate her.

As far as Mary was concerned, there were more important matters in hand as her Counter-Reformation began to gather pace. Unlawful books were now banned while priests who had taken wives were deprived of their livings and the first statute of repeal, although it had a difficult passage through parliament, wiped out much of what had been achieved by Cranmer over the previous twenty years. On Mary's

Bishop Bonner of London, principal heretic hunter and persecutor of Protestant martyrs for almost all of Mary's reign.

instructions, Edmund Bonner, the Bishop of London, began an investigation into the state of the church, an in-depth study that was intent on flushing out heresy wherever it was hiding. It was the start of the persecution.

With hindsight it is easy to take the traditional view and see Mary fighting a desperate and ultimately doomed rearguard action against hordes of fanatical Protestants who would go to the flames of Mary's fires rather than recant. But, even in the early stages of her reign, committed and dedicated Protestants were in the minority.

Church and religious practices were more important in the sixteenth century than today but, even then, for most people faith and belief came down to the simple matter of attendance at church services. Doctrine, theology and the intricacies of the actual service mattered little to the ordinary man or woman in the street or on the village green and were, by common consent, the business of those with greater education and authority. Dedicated Protestants, men and women prepared to die for their religion, were few and far between. Of course there were some but, as the later executions showed, these were in their hundreds not thousands.

As Mary settled in to her role as queen and as Catholic reformer, many of the leading evangelicals in England saw the writing on the wall and decided that discretion was certainly the better part of valour: 'The accession of a Catholic Queen was the signal for a stampede of Protestant leaders to escape to the continent—more than eight hundred exiles ... It was an exodus that Marian authorities did little to impede.'7

Gardiner, before his death, saw the exodus as an easy way out of the country's religious dilemma. Why bother to hunt down and arrest heretics when, with a little help and advice, they could be spirited abroad and cause problems elsewhere? There is no firm proof but it would be out of character for a man like Bishop Gardiner to miss such an easy opportunity to solve the problem of England's Protestants and the potential threat they posed. It is, as they say, a bankable hypothesis. Gardiner was the consummate political animal and it is more than likely that discreet warnings, invaluable leaks from unknown sources, were given to certain high-ranking Protestant leaders prior to roundups and arrests. Then it would be time to gather up whatever valuables they could lay their hands on and make a quiet departure.

Cardinal Reginald Pole

Reginald Pole became one of the chief advisers to Mary Tudor. A committed Catholic, he was born in 1500 in Staffordshire. His family was well connected, his maternal grandfather being George Plantagenet, Duke of Clarence. After studying at Magdalen College, Oxford, Pole went on to work for Henry VIII, and spending time in Paris attempting to negotiate a divorce from Catherine of Aragon. It was a short-lived alliance as Pole broke with Henry in 1531.

So bitter and outspoken was his condemnation of Henry that the English government even tried to have him assassinated. The attempt failed and Henry, unable to reach Pole, took terrible revenge on his family, imprisoning and executing those he could get his hands on.

Appointed cardinal in December 1536, Pole returned to England when Mary became queen and died just twelve hours after his sovereign.

43

For many who decided to remain in the country there was still one issue that could not be ignored: the way in which Mary had assumed power, swatting away the joint threat of Northumberland and his puppet-queen Lady Jane Grey, dismissing them as if they were no more than mice around a litter of bread crumbs, had been terribly effective but also terribly worrying.

There was, many felt, something divine about the way Mary had taken the crown, as if this was the way that God had intended things to happen. That belief caused many prominent churchmen and members of their congregations to promptly convert to Catholicism. It was a belief to which Mary herself subscribed, something that became almost a justification for what was to follow. For the people of England it was a more simplistic matter—Mary is the queen, we do what she tells us. If she wishes us to worship the old way, in the Catholic faith, then that, too, is fine. Many of those who now returned to the Catholic faith were genuine in their conversions. It would be wrong to say otherwise. Some, however, including people like the preacher Dr Henry Pendleton, were more self-interested: 'Pendleton, a corpulent man, vowed that "I will see the uttermost drop of this grease of mine molten away, and the last gobbet of flesh consumed to ashes, before I will forsake God and his truth." In the event, he himself soon conformed, became a notable Catholic persuader, preacher and disputant.'[8]

Pendleton was just one example of the opportunist at work but he was not alone. There were many like him in the country. They were easy to deal with; for the hard rump of Protestant support there would soon have to be greater and more reactionary solutions.

4. THE SPANISH MATCH

In his *Book of Martyrs* the writer and martyrologist John Foxe summed up one of the greatest fears of sixteenth-century England when he stated that there were people in the country who 'objected to Mary's being placed on the throne, on account of their fears that she might marry a foreigner, and thereby bring the crown into considerable danger'.[1] The idea of a foreign prince ruling over England was bad enough but the thought that in the event of the queen's death he might even take the throne for himself was abhorrent to most English people. It was perfectly possible, depending on the marriage agreement reached between the queen and the other parties, whoever they might be.

Henry VIII had effectively cut England off from the Continent, building a xenophobia that many would argue has never disappeared. The innate snobbery, or arrogance, of the English invariably led them to believe that no other people on earth were as fine and upstanding, as courageous and generous as them. So what did they need with any foreign prince?

When Mary became queen there appeared to be no reason to change that powerful policy of isolationism. The idea that the country would, if Mary chose to marry a foreigner, get dragged into Continental affairs—in particular the seemingly incessant series of wars between the Hapsburgs and the Valois dynasty of France—was the stuff of nightmares for men like the chancellor, Bishop Gardiner.

It was not as if everyone wanted her to remain chaste and

The Holy Roman Emperor and king of Spain Charles V, perhaps the most influential man in Europe during the reign of Mary Tudor.

Edmund Courtney, 1st Baron of Devon, who was the favourite option of Bishop Gardiner to marry the queen. Mary refused and later, having been involved in a plot against her life, finished his days in exile in Venice.

celibate. Everybody expected the queen to marry: apart from anything else, the stresses and strains of ruling alone, without support or assistance from a partner, were considered too onerous for a mere woman.

As ever in Tudor England, there was also the matter of providing an heir, someone who after Mary's death would secure the succession, take over the government of the country and further develop the return to Catholicism. Mary was thirty-seven when she came to the throne, almost past child-bearing age. The matter of finding a suitable husband was, therefore, of paramount importance.

For most people an English suitor would have been the best option but Mary's choices were limited as any prospective husband would have to be of both royal and Catholic blood. There was no notable contender in England, no great statesman who could be counted on to support the queen and give sensible advice. Mary quickly rejected Edward Courtney, the preferred choice of her Lord Chancellor, Stephen Gardiner. The old man had spent several years in the Tower with young Courtney, the grandson of Edward IV, and felt that he would be an ideal candidate. Not as far as Mary was concerned—she would marry no Englishman, she declared.

Dom Luis of Portugal and Maximillian, son of the emperor's brother, were candidates for a while but soon dropped out from the reckoning as they were neither as efficient nor as powerful as the position demanded. The Holy Roman Emperor, Charles V, even declared that he might consider marrying her himself but he was never really serious. Charles was old and worn out and would soon relinquish his various thrones to take a well-earned retirement. He did have a serious interest in Mary's projected husband, though, as events were soon to show.

Petitioned by a deputation from parliament urging her to choose an English spouse, Mary listened to what she considered an insolent address and then gave a dramatic and unequivocal response: 'Parliament was not accustomed to use such language to the Kings of England, nor was it suitable or respectful that it should do so ... She would choose according as God inspired her.'[2]

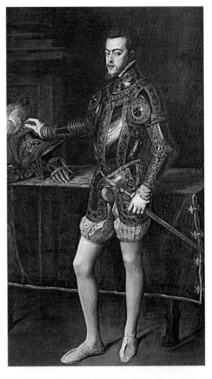

The parliamentary delegates were left stunned. No Tudor monarch had ever addressed them like that but it showed Mary's determination and her courage. No man—and certainly no institution like parliament—was ever going to browbeat her into making false assertions. She had done it once and had vowed then, never again. That left just one option, the preferred choice of both the emperor and Mary herself— Philip of Spain, the son of the emperor himself.

The emperor, Charles, had been one of the dominant and most effective players in European politics for many years. Old now and

Mary's eventual choice of husband, the largely ineffective Philip II of Spain.

well past his prime, he was still astute enough to see the value of the match between his son and the queen of England. It was made official when Simon Renard formally offered the hand of the Spanish prince—soon to be Spanish king—on 10 October 1553. Mary was delighted, not just for her own sake but for Charles's as well. The relationship between the two monarchs was intense, even if at long distance. The fact that Mary had been betrothed to Charles when she was little more than an infant meant nothing. Such betrothals were commonplace and invariably ended when there was no more need for the alliance.

But Charles had always supported Mary, offering a kind word when needed, promising military support should that be the prerequisite. Sometimes it left Bishop Gardiner wondering exactly what his role might be: 'Although she valued Gardiner's advice, she was naturally led to rely more on that of her cousin, the Emperor Charles V.'[3] Much as she admired Charles and his opinions, Mary was conscious of the limitations of time and distance between them. But marriage to Philip was a different matter.

For Charles it was a magical solution. The re-establishing of a Catholic regime in England had been a wonderful event, a recreation of the one true religion, and in

Mary and Philip shown together: she had the power, he had the glory.

many respects this alliance would be a further re-establishment of the relationship between England and Spain that had been created when Catherine of Aragon had been betrothed first to Arthur and then to Henry. It was not all altruism on the emperor's part. From a more pragmatic, political point of view, a Spanish prince on the throne of England would secure for Charles the sea route between the homeland of Spain and his provinces in the Netherlands. It would also mean that the French, always a thorn in the side of Spain, were suddenly encircled and a buffer placed between them and their new ally, Scotland.

The marriage of Mary Stuart (or Mary Queen of Scots as she was known) to the young Dauphin of France linked the two countries and promised serious logistical trouble for the emperor. This new marriage alliance between England and Spain was a potential way out of the problem. The importance of the betrothal for Charles and Philip could be measured by the concessions the emperor was willing to make to ensure that the marriage would actually take place: 'Philip was to hold the position of a mere consort. The courtesy title of King of England was to belong to him during the lifetime of Mary but no longer ... Should Philip and Mary have a child, the child's inheritance was to be the Netherlands and Franche Comte—at the expense of Philip's son (by his first wife), Don Carlos. Should Don Carlos die without issue the child of Philip and Mary should inherit the whole of the Spanish Empire.'[4]

When news of the proposed marriage leaked out there was considerable dismay in the country. The Spanish match was immediately unpopular. Englishmen simply did not like foreigners, perhaps Spaniards most of all, and many believed, as the king of France believed, that the alliance would simply drag England into war with her nearest neighbour.

It was a concern that occupied many a discussion, in the Commons, in the Royal Palaces and in the alehouses of the nation. As the marriage agreement shows, however, Mary had no intention of playing second fiddle to Philip and when the terms were made public at the beginning of 1554 it was clear that this was to be 'no Spanish takeover'.

While Philip was to help Mary in the governing of the country, he had limited power to make decisions. Importantly, he was to have no say in the appointment of state and Church officials. Mary alone retained that right and she was to choose only Englishmen. While there were to be no Spaniards in the English government, Philip was obliged to take a number of English diplomats and gentlemen of quality into his entourage.[5] Perhaps most important of all, by the terms of the Marriage Act, England was not obliged to support the emperor—or, indeed, Philip—in the event of war. It was reassuring for those like Gardiner who feared that a Spanish marriage would relegate the country to a mere dependency of the Hapsburgs.

Even while the arrangements were being made, trouble was brewing in the English countryside. Sir Thomas Wyatt, son of the poet of the same name, the man who supposedly introduced the sonnet into English poetry, was the prime mover. Together with a number of close friends from across England, he planned and implemented a rebellion against Mary.

The aims of the rebellion have never been totally clear. Wyatt himself was vague about what he intended, but preventing the Spanish marriage was certainly one issue. There was also the intention of disposing of Mary, marrying Princess Elizabeth to Edward Courtney and putting them, together, on the throne.

Whether or not Elizabeth was aware that her name had been dragged into the conspiracy is again open to conjecture. It would have been against all her natural instincts to let down her guard and allow herself to become implicated but she had spent long periods of her life in solitude and virtual imprisonment, so anything is possible.

The rising was planned for 18 March, the day that Philip was to begin his journey to England but long before that Wyatt had been betrayed to the queen and her government. With his intentions known to Mary and Gardiner, he raised his standard, ahead of time, in Kent and called on people to join him. His immediate followers were overjoyed but unfortunately for him, there were no simultaneous risings, as had been planned, across the rest of the country.

Desperate, now, and realizing his precarious position, Wyatt decided to take the offensive. He attacked and took Rochester on the Medway, then swung northeastward and marched on London. When he was met by a large detachment of City Whitecoats who had sallied out to oppose him, Wyatt declared that he was no traitor and was seeking only to defend the queen and the country from the Spanish—the Strangers as they were called. Many of the Whitecoats promptly deserted and joined him, the rest fled back into the city.

Mary, with the same courage that had enabled her to defeat Northumberland in 1553, immediately knew what she had to do. She rode to the Guildhall and there she addressed those who had stayed loyal to her or were wavering in their support. Her speech was stirring, in some ways a forerunner of Elizabeth's address to her troops at Tilbury during the invasion crisis of 1588. When Mary came to the potentially thorny issue of her marriage she made it crystal clear: marriage was for the purpose of leaving the English people with an heir: 'Yet if I thought this marriage would endanger any of you, my loving subjects, or the royal estate of this English realm, I would never consent thereto, nor marry while I lived.'[6]

The response was ecstatic. For several minutes cheering drowned out all other sound. People shouted with pleasure and one call above all others was constantly heard: 'God save Queen Mary and the Prince of Spain.'[7]

The following day Wyatt and his troops reached Southwark. The gates of London Bridge were closed to him and he immediately implemented a siege. It was a half-hearted affair without siege canons and engineers to design the entrenchments. If anything it was more like a blockade with Wyatt and his men preventing anyone from entering or leaving the city.

After three days, fearing attack from the rear, Wyatt abandoned the siege, headed west and crossed the Thames at Kingston. There was now real fear for the queen's safety. Advised to take a boat down the Thames and flee, Mary refused, remaining at Whitehall as Wyatt drew ever closer.

If it had been up to her she would have donned armour and fought at the head of her troops. She was carefully and delicately prevented from this dangerous but undoubtedly heroic course of action by her advisers. Her troops would have loved it but the gesture could, with one false shot or crossbow dart, have simply presented the throne to Elizabeth.

Over 20,000 citizens of London armed themselves and prepared for the attack. Wyatt mustered his forces in Hyde Park and once again Mary was urged to flee. Again she refused. Wyatt now led his troops along Fleet Street but finding Ludgate barred and protected by cannon he had no option but to retrace his steps. At Temple Bar Wyatt and his followers were attacked by troops loyal to the queen. The skirmish was short and sharp and by early evening Wyatt's forces were in disarray. Having no stomach for the fight, Wyatt had already surrendered, destined for imprisonment in the Tower.

Forty people were killed in the fighting, two of them Mary's soldiers, and that night the celebrations were long and hard, both in the high offices of state and in the taverns and alehouses of the city of London. The queen had, once again, led from the front in what transpired to be a fairly minor affair but which had always had the

The execution of Sir Thomas Wyatt after his failed rebellion against Mary and the Spanish marriage.

potential to explode into something considerably more dangerous. The display of courage by the queen was no more than people expected but this time it was different. Now she was driven, not by passion and desire for the right, but by ice-cold fury and determination.

There were no thoughts now of displaying clemency as she had done when claiming her throne; she was angry and knew that the citizens would stand for nothing less than revenge. That was fine, it fitted perfectly with her own ideas and intentions: 'Wyatt was executed and so were Lady Jane Grey and her husband, even though they had not taken part in the rebellion. Mary had learnt, like her father, that those who stood close to the throne were a constant menace, however innocent their intentions.'[8] Lady Jane's father, the Duke of Suffolk, had been involved in the rebellion.

Fictitious portrait called Margaret Tudor; after an unknown artist in the mid-19th century. (National Portrait Gallery NPG D13259)

That was enough for Mary. It was decision made and the hapless—and probably innocent—Lady Jane had to go.

Princess Elizabeth, who might have been involved but then again might not, was initially kept under quasi-arrest at the palace. There was little real evidence against her but it did seem as if she was aware of the projected rebellion. Among other bits of evidence it appeared that Wyatt's plan called for several of the houses owned by the princess to be fortified and held against attack.

As a result of this limited evidence Elizabeth was escorted to the Tower and for some weeks there was a real possibility that she might even be executed. When Sir Thomas Wyatt went to the block on 11 April he exonerated Elizabeth in a final speech to the crowd. Nothing could be proved against the princess, no matter how hard the inquisitors tried and in the end she was released and sent off to live quietly at Woodstock Palace in the country. For almost a year she was under virtual house arrest.

Thomas Wyatt's failed rebellion finally cleared the way for Mary's marriage. Before that could take place, however, she needed to know that she was safe. She needed to be clear that there was not another Thomas Wyatt out there, waiting to betray and attack her. Fear and the all-consuming insecurity of the adolescent girl had not left her.

Revenge was in the air and, in sweeping raids by government officials, hundreds of people were arrested and questioned; many were subsequently hanged and very few escaped punishment altogether.

It was the hard edge of Mary's anger—paranoia would not be too strong a word—and was not something the people had seen before. The repressed teenage emotion of Mary's personality, fuelled by fear and by the sheer incredulity that her subjects could even consider betraying her, had bubbled to the surface. It gave a clear indication to

Right: Innocent of any involvement in Wyatt's rebellion, Lady Jane Grey—the nine-day queen installed by Northampton in 1553—was considered too great a risk to survive.

Below: The execution of a teenage monarch, Lady Jane Grey goes to the block.

everyone that one crossed the queen at one's own peril. During the rising Mary had behaved with admirable courage and determination, just as she had done when her accession had been challenged by the Duke of Northumberland. Later, once the immediate issues had gone, insecurity and that peculiarly adolescent desire to hurt those who had hurt her came surging to the fore. There were many potential enemies to choose from—and God help those who came to bear the brunt of her anger. Her victory over Wyatt and his rebels was, Mary felt, yet another sign from God. It was, as Simon Schama has said, 'a sign that he approved her marriage'.[9] It gave her, she felt, licence to act.

What now took place was a minor persecution, a forerunner to the greater events still to come. Nobody who knew Wyatt or had spoken with him was ignored or safe from interrogation and soon the sight and smell of rotting corpses, left as a warning on the hastily erected gibbets of the city, had made many a stomach turn. It was a deliberate policy. Mary's desire for vengeance had not stopped with the killing of those who had opposed her: ordinary men, women and children had to see the consequences of rebellion and understand the foolishness of ever thinking they knew better than the queen.

It was not gentle persuasion; it was a threat, clear and simple.

Gradually the madness faded but the memories of Mary's ferocity remained. It did not seem to adversely affect her popularity and that May of 1554, as she formally dissolved parliament, her speech to the assembled MPs was interrupted several times by ribald shouts of 'God save the queen'.

And so to the wedding. Mary and Philip met for the first time just two days before they were joined in marriage. He had landed at Southampton on the afternoon of 19 July, armed with a set of instructions and guidelines drawn up by Ambassador Simon Renard.

Although advised to learn at least a few words of English, Philip did nothing of the sort and spent his first weekend in the country resting after his journey from Spain. When he and Mary did finally come face to face, in the gardens of the palace, they spoke in a mixture of Spanish, French and Latin.[10]

The marriage of Queen Mary and, as he became after taking his vows, King Philip.

The wedding ceremony took place at Winchester Cathedral on 25 July 1554. Despite fears of a possible demonstration against the Spanish, everything passed off well enough, which was just as well: considerable sums of money had changed hands to ensure exactly this result.

The only downside to the ceremony was the sudden deluge of rain that greeted the couple as they made their way out of the cathedral. It confirmed Philip's opinions of this cold, windswept and unhappy island resting on the northern rim of the known world. Mary was gorgeously attired in a gown of white satin and before the ceremony began Bishop Gardiner announced that the emperor had just ceded to his son the crown of Naples and his claim to the city of Jerusalem. Mary was now marrying not a prince but a king.

To begin with Mary was deliriously happy. In Philip, she was sure she had found someone who would support her in the onerous task of running the country. He was handsome and attentive and it seems that from an early stage of their marriage she had fallen deeply in love with him. For Philip, however, it was not the same. He certainly did not find her physically or sexually attractive. She was eleven years older than him and he called her his 'dear and beloved aunt'. That may have been in jest or even love-talk which both of them apparently enjoyed, but it was possibly not a sound basis on which to begin a healthy relationship between two people who hardly knew one another.

Whatever Mary and Philip felt about each other it soon became clear that the English people had no time for the Spaniards. They found Philip and his entourage arrogant and were intensely suspicious of people talking in a language they did not understand. The feeling was mutual, the Spanish regarding the English as beer-swilling ruffians, 'pink, white and quarrelsome', who were out to rob them whenever they could.

After a ten-day honeymoon in Winchester the newlyweds started

The White Tower, the most sinister part of the Tower of London where all the serious prisoners were kept.

back to London. After stopping at Windsor and Richmond they entered the city and were welcomed with a number of pageants put on by the citizens. They were plays and masques that Philip could neither understand nor appreciate. After taking the plaudits of the crowds they then retired to Whitehall to begin their married life together.

The marriage was not a success but Mary, consumed by love and convinced that Philip felt the same as her, could not see it: 'Nothing could dampen Mary's ecstasy. For the first time in her lonely life she believed she had someone she could depend on ... Now, with the help of God and Philip, she could set about cleansing the realm of the pollution of heresy.'[11]

That cleansing began on 30 November at Westminster with Cardinal Pole instituting the Statute of Repeal.

As Mary and Philip, queen and king of England, along with members of both houses of parliament knelt in front of him, Pole formally absolved England for the years of schism and restored the country to the Holy Catholic Church. Such a move could not have been imposed on the country by the Church alone. This could only have been possible had the people of England come forward and requested reconciliation with Rome.

Knowing the venal nature of the Commons was one of Mary's great concerns. In order to achieve such an agreement Pole, Gardiner and Mary had bargained with the members of parliament over the one remaining obstacle, ownership of monastic lands. There was no way of consulting with every man in the country—even if such a move was thought desirable which, of course, it was not— and parliament was therefore taken to represent the people of England. A deal was struck whereby men owning former monastic or church lands could 'without scruple of conscience, enjoy them, without impeachment or trouble by pretence of any General Council, canons or ecclesiastical laws, and clear from all dangers of the censure of the church'.[12] Ownership of monastic property was widespread and nowhere was it more obvious or rampant than in the two houses of parliament. The members, land owners from both ends of the spectrum, had greedily grabbed what was on offer, invariably at 'knockdown' prices. They guarded their newly acquired wealth with a ferocious sense of ownership. But with a deal struck and their recently acquired lands safely out of the grasp of the Church, members were happy.

Now the real business of Mary's restoration or Reformation could begin. Mary and men like Gardiner were determined to keep everything legal and almost without realising what had transpired, the people of England suddenly found that the groundwork had already been completed. Whatever their religious stance, there was now nothing that Mary's subjects could do to prevent the persecution. The instruments of restoration were already in place, the legal apparatus to allow what soon began to occur across the country having been almost slipped through parliament unnoticed. Most people were concerned more about the Statute of Repeal than any other legislation. It was, as many soon found out, a mistake.

The Statute of Repeal had been preceded by something that was considerably more significant for the queen and for the Catholic Church—and a lot more menacing for the people. It was an Act reviving the old heresy laws and it was, in effect, a death warrant for 284 men and women.

Burning at the stake was a popular method of execution across Europe. This one is taking place in Germany in the earlier days of the Reformation.

5. THE BURNINGS BEGIN

Beginning in the early months of 1555 Mary Tudor instituted a long-running series of executions that was more a statement of belief than the destruction of criminals and malcontents. The blood-letting was unparalleled in English history. It is impossible to exonerate Mary: she was a hands-on, direct ruler, like all Tudor monarchs, and as such she has to bear the brunt of blame. She instigated, she drove; she was the architect of what quickly became a reign of terror.

Martyrs at the stake. The illustration gives a clear indication of how the fires were built, bundles of faggots being stacked up around the bodies of the condemned.

The burning of heretics at the stake was a fairly common form of ritual punishment in the sixteenth century, one that was not confined only to Catholics or to England. Free expression in religious matters was unheard of with the result that tolerance was limited and compromise unknown.

In an age when abstract thinking was rare and God, the Devil, Heaven and Hell were seen as real, the fear of eternal damnation haunted the dreams of many. Physical punishment for heretical thoughts and behaviour was, therefore, crucially important for the church in this literal, one-dimensional era.

There had been many instances of heretic burning over the years and many means were used to dispatch them. In 1410, the former monk John Badby was burned at Smithfield in a wooden barrel.

John Badby, an early victim who was burned in a barrel.

Another heretic burned by Henry VIII, Richard Bayfield went to the stake in 1531 while Thomas More was Chancellor of England.

Even so-called 'saintly men' like Sir Thomas More were not above sending heretics to the fire. He was responsible for the burning of Richard Bayfield, a man who had worked closely with the Bible translator William Tyndale, in December 1531.

Mary's father, Henry VIII, had burned over sixty people at the stake—Catholics or those who refused to acknowledge his supremacy of the church. So the punishment was not unknown to the queen and her advisers. It was a violent age when burning people alive was just one end of the punishment spectrum. Traitors—and even imagining the monarch to be dead or speaking about him in the past tense could be considered an act of treason—suffered the gruesome punishment of hanging, drawing and quartering. Members of the nobility who were granted the largesse of simple beheading were lucky. As long as the executioner knew his job, it was at least quick.

Burning at the stake was neither quick nor merciful: it took time and many of the martyrs spent as much as forty-five minutes to an hour in the flames, burning slowly and painfully until death finally arrived. If the executioners were feeling merciful they might allow relatives of the victim to place tiny bags of gunpowder around the neck or in the groin of the condemned man or woman. When they exploded death would be virtually instantaneous but the flames had to first reach the gunpowder. Very few people died from smoke inhalation; most of them burned and there are numerous accounts of victims 'washing their hands' in the flames, although such actions might well have been an involuntary spasm, a final twitch of the nervous system as the victim died. Occasionally, spectators would take pity on the dying, as happened with Bishop Farrar in Carmarthen when a blow to the head ended his suffering. Mostly people just looked on as the martyrs burned.

Not that punishment was meant to stand alone. The aim was to persuade as well as punish and to this end Cardinal Pole was clear that quality Catholic preaching was required if England was to be effectively brought back into the Church. He meant general, everyday preaching in church and as well as at the execution; hardly what the condemned martyrs wanted to hear but certainly what they were going to get.

Religious tracts and books were also important in a century when the printing presses of the recently deceased Caxton and Wynkyn de Worde were beginning to make their presence felt.

Books were expensive to produce and to buy. It did not stop the rapid growth of the new printing industry. In 1548, just ten years after de Worde's death no fewer than 232 books were printed in England. In 1555, as Mary's heretic hunting really began to bite, the figure was 132, not including Protestant books that were produced in Europe and clandestinely smuggled into the country.[1]

All of this was a backdrop to the real drama that was taking place in Mary's life. In November 1554 she stopped menstruating and gained weight, afflicted by

Despite the fine gowns and jewellery, Queen Mary is already beginning to feel the strain of ruling the country and the reintroduction of the Catholic faith.

morning sickness. Mary was delighted. She was clearly pregnant, something that her doctors quickly confirmed. She did not need their opinions; she had felt the baby move inside her. Her desire to have a child was all-consuming and her belief that she was pregnant was unshakeable. She was not alone in that belief.

Parliament immediately passed an act declaring that Philip should become regent if Mary died in childbirth—a fairly standard precaution—and in April 1555 Princess Elizabeth was released from house arrest and brought to court to act as a witness to the birth. When Mary appeared in public she took great pains to stand side on to the crowd in order to show off her belly. She was supremely happy and everything, it seemed, was going to plan. And then the rumours began.

The queen was not pregnant, people whispered; it was merely a figment of her imagination. She had already given birth, commented others and the child was dead or had emerged as a mole. At one stage church bells across London were rung and bonfires lit to celebrate the birth of a young prince. The rumour mill was wrong and celebrations were immediately put on hold. Still people talked: the queen had miscarried, she had given birth to a monkey, she was bewitched, she was dead.

Philip—and he, more than anyone, should have known—actually doubted that his wife was pregnant at all. Mary became reclusive and deeply depressed. Finally, in the early summer her swollen abdomen receded and she began menstruating again. There was no baby and there never had been. It was a false pregnancy, probably fuelled by the queen's desperate desire for a child and by the relationship between her and her husband. That relationship was already cooling, at least on his side. Even ensconced behind the walls of Hampton Court Palace where she had gone for her confinement, Mary could not help hearing the muted laughter or see people whispering behind their hands. The ridicule was hard to bear and Mary decided that it had been God's punishment for her leniency.

It would not be taking too great a leap to suggest that the two major events of 1555—Mary's phantom pregnancy and the first of the Marian burnings—were linked. In 1555 there was no such thing as psychiatry and nobody has left records to say that it was or was not so. Much of the reasoning remains guesswork but knowing her character and the repressed nature of her personality it is at least educated guesswork. And it leads, inevitably, to the likelihood of the queen's need to lash out when she had been hurt or damaged in some way. Adolescent desires and emotions, mixed not just with the bitter rancour of the phantom pregnancy but also the shame of being mocked by her peers and by the common people, more than likely brought the concept of revenge to her mind once more. Someone would have to pay and there were numerous sitting targets out there just waiting to be attacked.

Archbishop Thomas Cranmer, a painting by an unknown artist soon after the death of Henry VIII. It is sometimes said that the length of his beard indicated his mourning for the king and his acceptance of the Protestant religion.

Although the burnings began in February 1555, punishment of those who did not conform had often been spoken about in Council long before that. For months there had been talk of exacting vengeance on the Protestants for the persecution endured during Edward's reign, despite the fact that only three Catholics—compared to the sixty of Henry's reign—had been hunted down or executed.

The knife edge of Mary's campaign against Protestants was the swathe of bishops who ruled over their sees with rods of iron. Given leave by the queen to hunt down heretics, they took to their task with a will; almost overnight they imposed what can only be termed martial law for religious offences and by the end of Mary's first year as monarch they were more feared than the sheriffs or magistrates who had control of civil law.

Heretics had always been a problem but, apart from the wholesale expulsion of Jews in 1290, there had never been a systematic persecution in England. Things were different now as arrests and confinements for Protestant beliefs doubled. Not everyone reached the execution stage. Many of those apprehended died of natural causes: 'Thomas Dolbe, who at the beginning of the reign, was apprehended for speaking against the idolatry of the Mass, and died in prison.'[2]

Natural deaths or not, the burnings were coming. Had Mary, three months into her supposed pregnancy, accepted—perhaps subconsciously—that the outcome of her claim to be with child would be negative? Maybe, just maybe, the subsequent burnings were little more than the furious lashing out of the repressed adolescent who has been frustrated in her desires and wishes. Or had she already decided, after events like Wyatt's rebellion, that enough was enough and that those Protestants who remained in England needed to be taught a lesson? It is supposition and trying to get inside the mind of Mary Tudor remains a process fraught with danger.

Either way, neither Mary nor Cardinal Pole had expected to burn so many. And they had certainly not intended that the executions would go on for so long. The earliest burnings were meant to shock, to bring recalcitrant Protestants to their senses, which is why, to begin with, the victims were men who were reasonably well known in their communities. And, of course, in those local communities were where they perished. These early martyrs were men of substance. People knew of them, respected them, and would be brought up short by the manner of their deaths. There was nothing personal in the process—except for Thomas Cranmer but he would come just a little later.

The facts are that the burnings began on 4 February 1555. Execution by burning at the stake was the ultimate punishment but it was intended to be used only if the accused refused to recant, one of the reasons that every execution was accompanied by a sermon from a notable clergyman. Even up to the point where the fires were lit and smoke began to billow across the crowd, recantations would have been accepted. By that stage, however, the 'heretic' had usually made his peace with God and was ready to die.

John Rogers, the first victim of Mary's persecution, went to the stake in 1555.

The first martyr of Mary's reign was John Rogers, Vicar of St Sepulchre's and Reader of St Paul's, who was burned at Smithfield on 4 February. Soon after Mary's ascension to the throne, he had preached at St Paul's Cross, a notable public space outside the cathedral of St Paul's where sermons were often given. His sermon and his message were clear, warning listeners to beware popery, idolatry and superstition, a direct challenge to Mary's belief system and the new regime.

Rogers, arrested and accused of heresy, defended himself so well that, at first, the charge was dismissed and he was allowed home. On the personal instructions of the queen, however, he was arrested again and placed under house arrest. Supervision of the man was lax and it would have been easy for him to have escaped and made his way to Germany, the spiritual home of Protestantism and, of course, the country where Martin Luther nailed his Ninety-five Theses to the door of the Castle Church, Wittenberg. Yet Rogers was a man of scruples and flight to the Continent would have meant leaving his wife and ten children without means to survive. He was determined to remain in London and continue to preach. Despite the order placing him under house arrest, Rogers was often out in the city and eventually his preaching began to get under the skin of the authorities. Eventually Bishop Bonner could take no more. He had Rogers arrested and committed to Newgate Prison where he was condemned to death for his heresy.

Rogers was soundly asleep when officials arrived to inform him that he would be burned that day, so much so that it took several attempts for the gaoler to wake him. His one request was that he should be allowed to speak to his wife but this was denied. Led to the place of execution, Mr Woodroofe, one of the sheriffs in charge of the burning, asked him if he would recant. He refused. 'Mr Woodroofe said, "Thou art a heretic." "That shall be known," quoth Mr Rogers, "at the Day of Judgement." "Well," said Mr Woodroofe, "I will never pray for thee." "But I will pray for you," said Mr Rogers.'[3]

In front of a huge crowd, he was committed to the fire and died, washing his hands in the flames as he burned. A short while before his execution a pardon was brought out to him, granting him freedom and life if he would only recant. He refused. Many in the crowd apparently wept and called for God to give Rogers strength. Afterward, when the fire had cooled, several people gathered together the ashes from his corpse, along with his bones, and wrapped them up for preservation. John Rogers had conducted himself with dignity and courage and nobody who

Papists in Europe burning Lutheran literature. (Hans Lilje)

witnessed his execution could have denied his faith. By refusing a pardon but, at the same time, praying for his killers he made an indelible impression on those who stood watching.

His execution was the start of a regular procession, sometimes several people going to the flames each day. With official policy being to execute heretics either in the district where they lived or, if they were churchmen, where they had officiated, meant that prisoners were often transported up and down the country. It is testament to their faith and courage that very few of them attempted to escape at such times.

John Hooper, former Bishop of Worcester and Gloucester, was one of the 'big names' of the Protestant Reformation. As such, he was one of the first to suffer martyrdom and followed Rogers to the flames in February 1555.

Arrested and imprisoned in the Fleet Prison in London, it was decided that he should return to Gloucester to die. Taken back to the West Country he was led out of his temporary lodgings in the city just after eight in the morning of 9 February. Again, he was offered a pardon if he would recant and when he refused the fire was lit with the order to dispatch him quickly. Unfortunately for Hooper the execution was neither speedy nor efficient. The faggots were green and the fire refused to kindle. The wind blew the flames away from him, burning only his legs and hair. A second fire was lit around his body but again only managed to burn his legs. In agony Hooper prayed for 'more fire'. A third fire was more effective, two bladders of gunpowder between his legs finally exploding. Yet still he remained alive: 'But when he was black in the mouth, and his tongue so swollen that he could not speak, yet his lips went until they were

Philip and Mary, anything but a happy couple.

shrunk to the gums: and he knocked his breast with his hands until one of his arms fell off, and then knocked still with the other, while the fat, water and blood dropped out at his fingers' ends ... Then immediately bowing forwards, he yielded up his spirit.'[4] Bishop Hooper had spent nearly an hour in the flames before he died. It was an agonizing death before a crowd of many thousand. But it did not put anyone off, not the executioners nor the spectators who had come to see blood.

The same day as Hooper went to the fire, two other men were also executed. A week later no fewer than six were dispatched on the same day. Included in these was John Laurence, a defrocked priest. Having been kept in shackles in his prison cell, he was too weak to walk and was burned at Colchester sitting in a chair. His children stood in front of him and prayed as he died.

In the summer of 1555 Philip left England. He told the queen that he would not be gone for long and even left many of his household staff behind him in an effort to convince her that his words were genuine.

Despairing of Mary's failure to produce an heir to the English throne, he went to the Low Countries to take command his armies in the continuing war with France. To everyone apart from the queen, the likelihood of a speedy return to England appeared highly improbable.

Mary was heartbroken at the parting, watching the departing Philip with tears streaming down her face. She wrote to him virtually every day and for a while he replied quite regularly. But he had a military campaign to run—that, at least, was his excuse—and gradually he began to write less and less. Slowly Philip's remaining household staff were withdrawn, the last of them leaving the country in December.

In October 1555 Charles V passed on the lordship of the Netherlands to his son. Four months later, in January 1556, he abdicated as king of Spain and Philip succeeded to his bithright, taking over the joint crowns of Castile and Aragon.

Perhaps the time was now ideal for Philip to make greater demands on Mary? He wrote suggesting that he should be crowned king of England in his own right, as opposed to being merely a consort, and even hinted that this was a good way to induce him back to Mary's side. She refused, knowing how strong the parliamentary opposition was to the Spanish influence. Not only that, she had heard of Philip's amorous dalliances in Flanders and was not best pleased. The couple had been parted for several months now and if distance had not exactly taken the edge off Mary's infatuation it did, somehow, give her the power to look at things with more objectivity than in the past. If Philip would not come back to her without condition, then Mary resolved to withdraw completely from the company of men and live out the rest of her life in quiet contemplation.

Meanwhile the burnings continued. The horror of the procedure began to impinge itself more and more on the impartial members of the population but, even so, people were not necessarily put off from attending a burning. In places like Canterbury, where the executions were almost a weekly event, it was highly likely that every single member of the community witnessed at least two or three burnings each year.

If Mary had hoped that the threat of martyrdom would cause potential Protestant martyrs to recant she was gravely mistaken. If anything the fires simply strengthened the resolve of many of the men and women they were meant to terrify. And there was more: 'In three years 220 men and 60 women died on Mary's bonfires. At first they alarmed, then they horrified people, and not just the Protestants or moderate Catholics. Before he died in November 1555, old Bishop Gardiner, Cranmer's arch-enemy, spoke strongly against them. Philip and some of his closest advisers were dismayed by Mary's increasingly fanatical ardour and predicted it would alienate the crown from the people.'[5]

Opposition from the Protestants Mary had expected but strictures from her own people, even her husband, were something else. As might

A somewhat romanticized engraving from Foxe's *Book of Martyrs* shows a small group of martyrs on their way to the fire, each of them carrying faggots of wood.

Bishop Farrar of St David's, one of only three men executed in Wales during Mary's reign.

be expected, it simply added to her fanaticism and made her surer still that she was acting on God's instructions.

The early arrests and prosecutions had taken place in the diocese of Edmund Bonner, Bishop of London, even if the executions themselves had often been carried out elsewhere. But as the weeks went by, the witch hunt—there can be no other phrase to describe it—spread like an infection to other areas. Kent, Essex and East Anglia all saw dozens of burnings and there were even executions in far-off Guernsey. London, of course, saw more than most and the name Smithfield, already renowned as a meat market, remains synonymous with the martyrs of Queen Mary.

One of only three men to be burned in Wales was Robert Farrar, Bishop of St David's, in the far west. Executed in the main square of Carmarthen he stood motionless, despite his obvious agony, until a man by the name of Richard Gravell struck him with his staff and killed him before the flames could do the rest of their work.

Rawlins White was another Welsh victim. An illiterate fisherman from Cardiff, his son had learned to read and write and every evening would spend time reading the Scriptures to his father. Using that knowledge, White had become something of a street-corner preacher, a gospeller, during the reign of Edward. He was a familiar sight in the alleyways and streets of Cardiff and in 1555 was, inevitably, brought before Bishop Anthony Kitchin of Llandaff—the only bishop to retain his position during the reigns of Henry, Edward and Mary—accused of heresy. Despite prayers for his conversion, White refused to recant and was sent to the Cockmarel Prison in Cardiff. He passed his time there singing hymns and saying prayers. For twelve months he waited. On the day of execution his wife and children were in the crowd, causing the old man to break down in tears. It did not break his resolve, however. His legs were consumed before the rest of his body which, held in place by strong chains, simply toppled over into the flames and he died. His last words were, 'O Lord, receive my spirit.'[6]

White was a simple man who had caused little harm but now it was not enough to arrest those who gave anti-Catholic sermons or who refused to take Mass. Now villages, towns and houses had to be searched to find incriminating evidence. Dedicated heretic hunters specialized in the practice. In a few short months England had become something of a police state, a country where fear ran riot and men and women really did listen in trepidation for the midnight knock on the door.

The first woman to go to the flames was Margaret Polley from Pembury who died at Tunbridge Wells on 17 July 1555. She had stated that there was no mention of the Catholic Church in the Bible and denied the 'Real Presence' in the Mass. Refusing to take back her words she was, inevitably, found guilty and sentenced to burn.

A memorial to Cardiff fisherman Rawlins White. The memorial can be found on the wall of a department store on St Mary's Street in the city, the site of the execution.

At Polley's execution local farmers brought cart loads of cherries to sell to the eager crowd.[7] A day out was clearly something not to be missed and neither was the chance to make a few pennies. Selling fruit at executions quickly became a regular practice in the county of Kent.

It was not unusual to burn women at the stake, more often than not for crimes like witchcraft, but now the prospect of regular burnings provided spectators with more than a little titillation and excitement.

Margaret Polley was soon followed by a number of other women, including Alice Benden of Staplehurst who was denounced as a heretic by her own husband. Also disowned by her father, Benden spent nine weeks in prison during which time she was allowed no change of clothes and fed only on bread and water. When finally led out for execution she was 'a most piteous and loathsome creature to behold'. Alice refused to recant, believing that if the authorities could treat any human being in this way then they were surely nothing to do with the God she worshipped.[8]

Many of those Protestants who did not flee or convert were driven underground in the early days of the persecution. Rose Hickman and her husband Anthony, a

The Martyrdome of Margery Polley.

Margaret Polley was the first woman martyr of Mary's reign, burned at Tunbridge Wells in 1555.

wealthy merchant, were living in London when the burnings began. While keeping up appearances by attending Mass, they immediately set up a secret prayer room in their house where anyone could come to read the gospel and pray. This went on for some time but eventually they became alarmed by the growing radical nature of the persecution, closed down their prayer room and sought refuge in Antwerp.[9]

The Hickman's were not alone in holding illicit prayer meetings and even funding Protestant clergy to flee the country. But as the activities of Mary's heretic hunters and bishops really began to bite, it took raw courage and absolute belief to ignore the flames of the fires at Smithfield. Fewer and fewer people were that brave.

By the autumn dozens of martyrs had gone to the fires but the courage of the Protestants had impressed everybody and Mary and Cardinal Pole were beginning to realize that some big gesture was now called for.

6. EVEN THE ARCHBISHOP

One of the criticisms of Marian persecution has always been that it was aimed at 'the little man', people like Rawlins White and Margaret Polley, allowing many of the important figures in the Protestant Church to go scot free. Those who had the means to escape, including many of the lay leaders of the church, fled to the Continent in the early days of Mary's reign. It was far easier for a man or woman of substance, people like the Hickmans, to find the money and the opportunity to escape or hide than it was for the itinerant labourer or subsistence farmer.

Consequently, the roll call of martyrs from Mary's reign includes just nine who were listed as gentlemen. Approximately a quarter of those executed were from the clergy and the rest, the vast majority of the victims, came from the lower sections of society—weavers, fishermen, carpenters and so on: 'None of these men could, by rea-son of their very insignificance, be a real threat to Mary's Church. They were the representatives of the common people.'[1]

Clinging to the hope that the threat of burning at the stake might yet bring forth recanta-tions, Mary, Pole and Bonner retained the belief that one or two big successes might still swing the balance. The four most significant figures in Edward's Reformation had been bishops Hooper, Latimer and Ridley and, of course, Archbishop Thomas Cranmer.

Hooper had already gone to the fire in February but his cour-age at the point of death and the ineptitude of his executioners had not had the desired effect. With Hooper gone, the hope of

One of the 'big names' of the Protestant movement in England, Bishop Hugh Latimer was burned in October 1555.

Nicholas Ridley, former Bishop of London, was burned beside Latimer on 16 October.

the government was that one of the three, if not all of them, would recant. If not they would burn as surely as John Hooper.

If Mary harboured hatred for one man, an emotion that overrode her desire for revenge, it was Thomas Cranmer. She blamed him for the destruction of her parents' marriage and for taking her countrymen into the realms of heresy. She relished the thought of sending him to the stake but Cranmer could wait. The tension and the stress he was bound to suffer as he watched others die, Mary felt, only made the pleasure of taking him to task so much greater.

Hugh Latimer came from Leicester and at the age of just fourteen enrolled at Cambridge University. Converted to the Protestant cause during the reign of Henry VIII, he was accused of heresy by Cardinal Wolsey and was actually imprisoned in the Tower when Henry died. Released, he began preaching again and was elevated to the position of Bishop of Worcester. Even before Mary was crowned, he had a premonition that he would suffer martyrdom for his faith. He was arrested and taken to London, travelling past the chilling and charred remains of the fires at Smithfield. He smiled at his captors and commented that the place had long been 'groaning for him'.[2] He was imprisoned in the Tower for several months before being transferred to Oxford along with Ridley and Cranmer.

Nicholas Ridley came from Northumberland. Like Latimer he was educated at Cambridge and became head of Pembroke College. After time spent as the personal chaplain of Henry VIII, he was made Bishop of Rochester by Edward VI and then Bishop of London. Marked down by Mary as an obvious target for arrest, he was imprisoned immediately she came to power, and thrown into the Tower of London. Transferred to the Bocardo Prison in Oxford, Ridley was eventually taken out and lodged with a family by the name of Irish where he remained for nearly twelve months. Deprived of contact with men such as Cranmer and Latimer, he consoled himself by writing long letters to supporters and fellow Protestants.

Having refused to recant, both Latimer and Ridley were found guilty of heresy and condemned to death. On 16 October they were escorted to the place of execution opposite Baliol College. Cranmer, now alone in the Bocardo, was brought out of his

The execution of Latimer and Ridley at Oxford. Cranmer watches from the tower on the extreme right of the engraving.

cell and installed at the top of a tall tower where he would have an unimpeded view of the proceedings.

Dr Richard Smith preached a sermon that lasted considerably longer than anyone would have liked. Both the condemned requested the right of reply but this was denied. They were then led into the fir pit and strapped to a single stake while faggots and kindling were piled up around their bodies. The brother of Bishop Ridley tied bags of gunpowder around the necks of the two men, in order to quicken their end, and, as Cranmer watched—to encourage him to recant—the final proceedings began: 'A lighted faggot was now laid at Dr Ridley's feet, which caused Mr Latimer to say "Be of good cheer, Ridley, and play the man. We shall this day, by God's good grace, light up such a candle in England as I trust will never be put out."'[3] Latimer died quickly, his body engulfed by the flames. Ridley, on the other side of the fire, took longer. The fire burned only very slowly through the faggots that had been piled up around him with the result that while his legs burned, the flames did not rise higher and so could not reach the gunpowder tied to his neck. 'I cannot burn,' he was heard to cry in his agony but, eventually, after more wood was heaped onto the fire the flames reached the gunpowder. It exploded and, mercifully, Ridley finally succumbed.[4]

Cardinal Pole always placed great emphasis on persuading heretics to recant or convert rather than have them burned alive. It did not always work but when it did the results were usually rewarding: 'The most spectacular outcome of this policy came in the summer of 1556, when Edward VI's tutor and one of the key figures in the Protestant diaspora in Europe, Sir John Cheke, was kidnapped and brought to England where handpicked theologians under Pole's direction argued him into submission.'[5] The very idea of kidnapping religious leaders might seem more of a twenty-first century phenomenon than something out of the 1550s. Yet it gives an indication of the importance of men like Cheke and of the way religion was such a significant and compelling part of life in the sixteenth century. Whether or not Cheke's conversion was genuine, it was a huge blow to Protestantism across Europe. From the moment he renounced his heretical beliefs Cheke was obliged to accompany Bishop Bonner as he sat in judgement at various heresy trials across the length of Britain. He was, apparently, instrumental in gaining recantations from around thirty accused men.

The one person Pole could not save was Thomas Cranmer. Reviled by the queen, Cranmer's fate was sealed the moment Mary came to the throne. He could, and perhaps should, have fled to the Continent. Whether it was bravery, a sense of invulnerability or a need to carry on God's work, Cranmer was never one to take the easy way. He decided to stay.

A precocious youth, Thomas Cranmer had been educated at Cambridge where he became a fellow at Jesus College. He married and, as a result, was forced to give up his fellowship. He took up lodgings for his wife with a relative at the Dolphin Inn while he became Reader at Buckingham College. He rose steadily through the ranks of Henry's religious administration until on the death of Dr Warham, then Archbishop of Canterbury, Cranmer was appointed as his replacement. Though he received confirmation of this appointment from the Pope, he always maintained that he acknowledged no other authority than the king's.

On his succession to the throne, Edward maintained Cranmer as archbishop, using him to further develop the Reformation. Unfortunately, the death of Edward and the coming of Mary placed the archbishop in an invidious and highly dangerous position. Cranmer believed in the divine right of monarchs and so, while he was totally committed to the Protestant Church, he also supported Mary as queen. No matter what she thought of him and of his actions in the past, no matter how many martyrs she had burned at the stake, Cranmer still accepted her as the rightful monarch. He was in a dilemma, the demands of his conscience clashing with his belief in royal supremacy. There can be little doubt that in the months ahead this unenviable confusion was to play an important part in his actions. At the end of 1553 Cranmer was

The trial of Archbishop Cranmer.

called to explain himself in the Court of Star Chamber. He was later attained at a
meeting of parliament and in November 1554 he stood accused of treason.

The trial was to be held under papal jurisdiction. As Archbishop of Canterbury,
Cranmer received an order to appear in Rome to answer charges of heresy. It was an
impossible summons of course: even had he been free he would, he said, be too poor
to travel to Italy and employ an advocate on his behalf.[6] He was tried in absentia and
found guilty, whereupon he was deprived of his archbishopric and permission was
granted for his execution. Mary wanted her pound of flesh, however, and desperately
needed to see Cranmer condemned by his peers. In February 1556 a new commission
headed by Edmund Bonner, sat in judgement at Oxford. The result was a formality.

On 14 February 1555 Cranmer was publicly degraded by Bishop Bonner. Degrading
was a formal ceremony. In Cranmer's case he was first dressed in his archbishop's garb, then his priestly vestments. Slowly and with great ceremony these were
stripped from him and replaced with what were little more than rags and an old
gown. His head was shaved and then came the strangest of all the ritual punish-
ments: 'The hands were scraped with a knife to remove the holy oil with which they
had been anointed. The scraping could be done either gently or roughly. Protestants
alleged that Bonner tended to do it roughly whenever he took part in a degradation
ceremony.'[7] With Cranmer, Bonner was particularly harsh. This was no ordinary degradation, no ordinary execution either, and there was a point to be made.

After his ritual humiliation Cranmer was handed back to the civil authorities for confinement in the Bocardo. No longer the archbishop, nor even a member of the clergy, Cranmer spent lonely days and nights incarcerated when he had nothing but his faith to console him. Despite this, prison had little effect and so the authorities decided to try the opposite tack. Sent to the house of the Dean of Christchurch, he was afforded every conceivable luxury and treated with great courtesy, like an important visitor. Cranmer, now sixty-six and in poor health, was confused and disorientated by such kind and unexpected treatment after the privations of the Tower and the Bocardo. During this period, under significant and repeated pressure from the authorities and despite knowing that his fate was sealed whatever he might do or say, Cranmer signed a number of recantations or submissions. In the first of these he declared that he accepted the authority of the Pope because the queen, and her husband King Philip, ordered him to do so. It was a statement that fitted with his belief in the sovereignty of Mary.

The fifth recantation was the significant one. In this document, made just a few days before his execution, Cranmer accepted full papal supremacy, acknowledged the truth of transubstantiation and agreed that there was no solution outside the Catholic Church. It was an amazing climb-down for the architect of English Protestantism but old, alone and frightened he was probably hoping that the statement would save his life. If so, it was a forlorn hope. The recantation was the sign of a broken man, a

Cranmer's execution on 21 March 1556. His right arm is outstretched toward the flames, creating the legend of the hand that signed the recantation burning first.

sweeping confession of sin that took away his dignity and, at that stage, looked like handing Mary and Pole the victory they so desperately craved. If this did not destroy the foundations of the Protestant faith, nothing would.

The original date for Cranmer's execution, 7 May, was postponed. By recanting he should have been saved from the fire altogether but Mary's hatred was too great. She decided to ignore Cranmer's change of heart and the new date for the execution was set for 21 March 1556. This time there was to be no delay. The day was wet and the pre-execution sermon, usually given in front of the stake, was delivered before a packed congregation in the University Church of St Mary's. It had been arranged that Cranmer would give his final recantation, his seventh, verbally after the usual sermon. As expected, once the death sermon was finished he made his way to a raised dais at the front of the church, gazed out at the citizens who had come to see him die and began: 'I renounce and refuse as things written with my hand, contrary to the truth which I thought in my heart, and written for fear of death, and to save my life if it might be.'[8]

There was an immediate uproar in the church. This was certainly not what the authorities had expected or wanted. This was Cranmer going back on his recantations and proclaiming that his statements had been given in the hope that they would save his life. With difficulty, officials quietened the congregation. Cranmer had not finished, not by a long chalk: 'For as much as my hand offended, writing contrary to my heart, my hand shall first be punished; for may I come to the fire, it shall be first burnt.'[9]

That might have shocked those in authority and the people who had packed into the church to see him cringe in the face of death but there was more to come. His last words, when they were finally uttered, were more chilling. The message was short and damning and while there were some in the church who did not hear, the words and the meaning were soon hissed to everyone in the congregation. Cranmer was manhandled off the dais before he could drive the nail fully into Mary's heart. Nevertheless this final condemnation, shouted out as he was bundled away, sent the world spinning and caused an explosion of horror that rang in the air for weeks afterward: 'As for the Pope, I refuse him as Christ's enemy and Anti-Christ, with all his false doctrine.'[10]

Amidst utter chaos, Cranmer was yanked forcibly from the dais. But his words had been heard. With little care for his person, guards dragged him out of the church and hurriedly marched him to the place of execution, the same spot where Latimer and Ridley had met their deaths some weeks before. He approached the stake calmly and with resignation: 'Coming to the stake with a cheerful countenance and willing mind, he put off his garments with haste, and stood upright in his shirt ... His friends sorrowed for love; his enemies for pity; strangers for a common kind of humanity, whereby we are bound one to another.'[11]

As he was fastened to the post with an iron chain, Cranmer cried out, 'Unworthy right hand' and when the fire was well lit and the flames began to creep up his body the archbishop, true to his word, plunged his right hand into the midst of the fire. Despite what must have been excruciating pain, he held his hand in the flames until it was burned to a cinder. After that he died quickly, murmuring, 'Unworthy right hand' over and over like a mantra or a prayer. Otherwise did not move or give his executioners the pleasure of seeing him in pain. He died knowing he had found his true redemption.[12]

The death and martyrdom of Archbishop Thomas Cranmer.

What should have been the greatest success of Mary's heresy campaign had ended in failure. Word of Cranmer's final moments soon spread across the country and into Europe, making him the chief martyr, a man who had been tempted—as Christ had been tempted—but then saw the true way ahead and took it, regardless of his fate. For Mary it was a disaster. As planned, she had the man in the palm of her hand but her hatred of Cranmer was too intense and she had allowed him to slip away. As Cardinal Pole knew only too well, Cranmer should have been allowed to live after his many recantations and allowed to slip into obscurity. Denying him an audience had been Pole's idea: deny him an audience and he would soon be forgotten.

The day after Cranmer's execution Dr Cole—who had given the pre-execution sermon on the 21st—denounced the former archbishop in St Mary's, the same church where the drama of the previous morning had taken place. The recantations were later bound together and printed in book form with Cranmer's expected speech rather than the one he actually gave as the final chapter. It was all damage limitation and it fooled few.

The Martyrs Memorial in Oxford, outside Baliol College on the exact spot where Latimer, Ridley and Cranmer were burned.

Above: Another view of Cranmer's execution, this one from Foxe's *Book of Martyrs*.

Left: A burning gets under way at Tynedale.

7. EXCOMMUNICATE

Cranmer was dead but Mary could not help thinking that he had escaped the ridicule and the condemnation he so richly deserved. The sad fact was that both ridicule and condemnation were actually there, readily available, until Cranmer was allowed to recant his recantations. He went to his death with a dignity and a fortitude that contrasted greatly with his previous servile declarations and that served only to infuriate the queen.

Cranmer's demise had not, as Mary hoped, put the final nail into the Protestant coffin. If anything it had achieved only the opposite effect, further alienating the people of England from the Catholic regime—as Philip of Spain had predicted—and denigrating the personality of Mary Tudor. The epithet of Bloody Mary dates from this period more than from any other.

From the joy and acclaim that met Mary's accession just a few years before, the burnings—and Cranmer's in particular—had put an unbridgeable distance between the queen and her subjects. Her paranoia and outbursts of adolescent anger, combined with a growing degree of isolation from the public stage, simply added to the distance.

It is hard not to see Mary's regular withdrawals from public view, never permanent or long lasting, as adolescent sulking whenever she was frightened or not getting her own way—a sad reflection on the woman who, in the face of mortal danger, was capable of the most amazing acts of courage and strength. She needed a Thomas Cromwell or a Cardinal Wolsey to advise and support her. Above all she needed a husband who loved and understood her. She did not need Philip II of Spain.

Burnings continued with sickening regularity. Crowds at the executions were made up of cosmopolitan groupings. From vengeance-driven Catholics to friends and supporters of the victims—as well as a hefty proportion of thrill-seekers looking for entertainment—there were sometimes upward of five or six thousand people present at a burning.

The fun-seekers had little personal involvement with the condemned man so that even someone as devout and well considered as Rawlins White was met by shouts of 'Burn him!' and 'Light the fire!' as he was led to the stake.

Although the behaviour of the crowds at executions was generally good (apart from catcalls) there were exceptions: 'When Christopher Wade was burned outside Dartford in the summer of 1555, a large crowd assembled to watch, but evidently in holiday rather than sympathetic mood … When Wade attempted to shout down the

Catholic preacher stationed near the pyre, some of the bystanders pelted the condemned man with faggots, wounding him in the face'[1]

By the summer of 1556 attitudes were beginning to change as people found themselves increasingly appalled by the cruelty and the spectacle of men and women screaming in agony as they died in the flames. The voyeurs were still there but, as might be expected, their allegiance was competing with cock-fighting, boxing and bear-baiting.

Far from terrifying Protestants into recanting or warning ordinary, conforming citizens what could happen to them if they fell from the straight and narrow, the burnings simply hardened the hearts of many. The consistent bravery of the heretics was what people talked about in the alehouse at night or as they sheltered from the wind and rain on the open heathland. The thirty or so men that Sir John Cheke had brought back to God had somehow managed to slip into obscurity. Brutality had always been more appealing to the 'great unwashed' and Cheke's efforts were anything but brutal.

Catholicism, the 'old religion', had clearly not lodged itself in the hearts and minds of the English nation and sometimes, to people who were still superstitious and literal in their beliefs, it seemed as if God himself was against them. And against their sovereign who had laid this trouble on them.

The winter of 1555/6 saw the worst rains in living memory. Livestock drowned and the land was saturated. It resulted in poor harvests and in parts there were serious food shortages, and famine. It was God's judgement, people whispered.

Philip II of Spain and, until Mary's death, king of England.

Dislike of the Spanish had not gone away either and there were rumours that Philip was to be formally crowned king—with all the powers that entailed. The cost of such an exercise, people said, was to found in yet another tax or levy. The mood of the people was ugly and there was open talk of rebellion. At one stage the Queen's Council even closed the gambling houses of London. There was fear that the treason so often spoken about and brewed to perfection in establishments like the gambling and dance halls of the capital might escalate into actual violence.

In the New Year of 1556 the pace of persecution quickened and the Council decreed that spectators at executions would no longer be allowed to offer help or praise to the heretics. At the same time, because of the contemptuous way it was treated—and generally refused—the queen's pardon was no longer to be offered, as it had been since the burnings began, to men and women at the stake.[2]

The rumbling dissatisfaction finally erupted into open rebellion that March. It was led by the cousin of Mary's old enemy, the Duke of Northumberland, Sir Henry Dudley, with the knowledge and complicity of the French government. Its aim was

Pope Paul IV who, in his own way, caused as much confusion and chaos in the Christian world as Henry VIII.

to replace Mary with her half-sister Elizabeth and involved robbing the Exchequer of £50,000. The plot was discovered and revealed to Mary's agents but Dudley who was in France negotiating for troops, escaped arrest.

Two of the other conspirators, John Throgmorton and Richard Uvedale, were immediately arrested and suffered the fate of hanging, drawing and quartering at Tyburn. Eventually they were joined on the scaffold by a further eight insurgents. The plot itself was fairly insignificant and easily defeated but it terrified Mary. She retired from public view, spending her days in seclusion and filling the palace with vigilant soldiers. Dudley's plot also revealed the duplicity of the French. Hatred of Spain, rampant in England, was mirrored in France and it was clear that the French king would do anything to reduce the threat on his own position.

In the meantime Mary needed support, the type of support only a husband and a consort could give. She needed Philip but despite tears, temper tantrums and letters by the score, Mary's distant husband showed no inclination to return to England. And then, when Mary and Cardinal Pole thought things could get no worse, they did. In May 1556 a new pope was elected. Pope Paul IV was a devious and suspicious individual, looking everywhere for double-dealing and treachery—even if it was not there. Heresy, he felt, was rampant across Europe and had to be wiped out.

The new pope was also violently anti-Spanish and immediately began to consider ways of trying to free Italy from Spanish tyranny. Charles V had invaded and imposed military rule on the country, and on the Pope after capturing Rome some years before. It had gone on long enough, Paul felt.

Philip, the son of Charles, was now effectively king of Spain, England and Italy, perhaps the most admired man in the whole of Europe. He was, therefore, a logical target for Pope Paul's machinations. When the Pope negotiated an alliance with France, Philip was furious and immediately sent his best general, the Duke of Alba, back into Italy to occupy the Papal States.

Pope Paul's response was swift. He excommunicated Philip and immediately removed the papal representatives from all of his kingdoms. That included England where Cardinal Pole was deprived of his legateship and ordered to return to Rome. There, before the Inquisition, he would answer charges of heresy and of subscribing to Lutheran views. Mary suddenly found herself in the most bizarre situation imaginable: 'Mary, a devout daughter of the Catholic Church, was in the invidious position of being married to an excommunicate husband and having her chief adviser a suspect heretic.'[3]

She had recently lost the services of Bishop Gardiner when the old man had died at the end of the previous year; she did not want to lose Pole as well. She ordered him to ignore the Pope's summons, an act that would have been unthinkable just a few months before. Now it showed how vulnerable she was feeling. And as for

Philip, he was her husband and she would support him like any good wife in her position would do.

On 30 March 1557 Philip at last returned to England. He came with all of the pomp and ceremony that royalty expected. Church bells rang and dances and pageants were held in his honour. Mary was overjoyed but her pleasure was marred by the real reason for her husband's return. Philip's strategy was to relieve pressure on his Spanish armies in Italy by opening up another front from his base in the Low Countries. That would effectively split the French forces, forcing them to fight on two fronts. It was a sound military strategy. There was only one problem: he was virtually bankrupt and could neither pay for troops nor fund what was likely to be a long and costly war. He needed the support of his queen and that of her country.

Mary was more than happy to give that support; the Privy Council was not. Consequently, they decided that they could not fund or contribute to the campaign, reminding Philip that the marriage agreement expressly forbade him to involve England in any war he might decide to wage. Mary, furious at having her will challenged, screamed at them—as ever, like a thwarted teenager—and demanded that they reconsider. But they did not change their minds.

Finally, as the court began to break up for the Easter celebrations at Greenwich, Mary summoned the councillors to come, one by one, to her room and in a series of private audiences cajoled, bribed and threatened them with a wide range of consequences—from land forfeiture to death—if they would not support her husband in his war.

The threats did not go unheeded but still the Privy Council refused come out openly in support of war. However, in light of Mary's threats, the Council declared that it was prepared to offer money and soldiers but that was all.

Mary and Philip now had a lucky break. On 23 April a Protestant exile, Thomas Stafford, landed and captured Scarborough Castle on the Yorkshire coast. He had a tiny army of just a hundred men, comprised of English Protestants and, crucially for Mary, French mercenaries. He had come, Stafford said, to depose Mary and return the country to the Protestant faith.

It was far from an efficient or dangerous invasion and it was only a matter of weeks before Stafford was defeated and Scarborough Castle retaken. Stafford was sent to London, executed for treason and disappeared from the pages of history. But the effect of French soldiers landing on English soil galvanized the Privy Council into action. On 7 June 1557 England declared war on France. Philip had got his wish. Early in July Mary accompanied him to Dover and, at dawn one morning, stood on the quayside as he took ship for the Low Countries. She might have suspected but did not know that they would never see each other again.

Scarborough Castle, captured by an invading force of French mercenaries in 1557. The ramifications of its capture were far greater than the event itself.

Over a thousand English foot soldiers and knights made the journey across the Channel, under the command of the Earl of Pembroke who had some limited successes in the early days of the campaign. Supported by the Spanish, he captured the town of St Quentin; the victory was received with much rejoicing in the English court. But it was to be something of a false dawn as the war quickly turned into a disaster for Mary. As far as armies in the sixteenth century were concerned winter was traditionally a time of restraint and rest with no campaigning and certainly no fighting. The French, however, decided that in the winter of 1558 the marshes around Calais would be frozen, allowing them easy access to the town.

Calais was England's last possession in France, of what had once been the mighty Plantagenet empire. It had been ruled by kings like Henry V and Richard the Lionheart; it had been fought over throughout the Hundred Years War and it was now the lone outpost. As such, Calais had significance and a symbolism far beyond its size and military value.

The town might have been important but its defences had been neglected during the reigns of both Edward and Mary. Walls and towers had crumbled under the combined effects of French winters and unpardonable neglect. The garrison was

The siege of Calais and its capture, January 1558.

below strength and short on vital supplies. When the French army appeared before the town on New Year's Day 1558 it was clear that the defenders would not be able to hold out for long. On 7 January the castle was captured and Lord Wentworth, the commander, surrendered. In many respects it was a blessing in disguise as England's fortune and future lay in territories far across the seas but to Mary it was yet another blow that she neither needed nor deserved. Calais had been an English possession since 1347 and it symbolized England's greatness, at least to Mary. Now it had gone. And a small piece of her country's standing and position in the world had gone with it.

Whether the queen ever made the statement that was later attributed to her—'When I die, cut me open and you will see Calais engraved upon my heart'—is a moot point. It is a good story but how accurate it is remains unknown. She certainly regretted its loss but attributed the defeat to lack of Spanish support and to poor military judgement on the part of her husband.

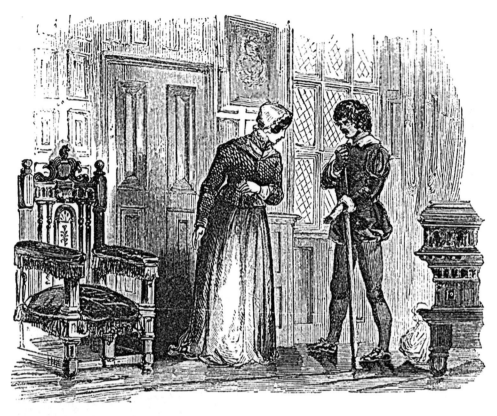

Above: As someone who was clearly more biased towards Protestants than Catholics, Princess Elizabeth was at the centre of numerous plots against Mary. It is doubtful if she knew much about them but, as a consequence, she spent much of Mary's reign under house arrest.

Left: Simon Renard, the imperial ambassador, who warned Mary not to trust her half-sister Elizabeth.

The reality is that she had more pressing matters to attend to. To start with, Pole had not had his legation reinstated. As far as Pope Paul was concerned he had not yet appeared before the Inquisition and until that happened he was not prepared to alter his stance. He now suggested that Cardinal Peto, an eighty-year-old former friar, should replace Pole as Papal Legate.

The fact that Peto turned down the invitation due to infirmity mattered little. It was the sleight that hurt Mary's feelings and she desperately wanted Pole reinstated. When peace between Philip and the Pope was agreed, one of the terms of the treaty was that Pole should be allowed to regain his legation.

PAVLVS · IV · PAPA · NEAPOLITANVS·

Pope Paul IV.

It never happened and eventually death, for both Pole and the queen, overtook any decisions the Pope might have been considering.

While continuing to mouth her devotion to the papacy, relations between Mary and Rome—particularly with Pope Paul IV—continued to deteriorate. For a while there was a fear that diplomatic relations might be broken off entirely. In the end it came to nothing and while the Pope might have welcomed Mary's successor Elizabeth as someone who appeared to be more favourable than her sister, it was a short honeymoon period. More than anything else, however, the religious and political distance between Mary and the Bishop of Rome gave a clear indication of how her reign and her own concept of herself had deteriorated. It was a far cry from the heady days of her accession to the throne.

Martin Luther and the Reformation

Born on 10 November 1483, Martin Luther was the cornerstone and originator of the Reformation that caused such chaos and religious wars across Europe in the sixteenth century. He was a professor of theology, a monk and a composer, one of the most influential men of his time.

The seminal moment in Luther's life came in 1517 when he nailed his Ninety-five Theses to the door of the Castle Church in Wittenberg, disputing the traditional Catholic views on matters like indulgences. Called to answer for his views at the Diet of Worms, Luther was unrepentant and while he wanted to reform rather than destroy the Catholic Church, it marked the beginning of the Protestant religion.

Excommunicated by Pope Leo X and declared an outlaw by the Holy Roman Emperor Charles V, Luther's views were debated and discussed across the known world. While monarchs like Henry VIII of England were, to begin with, condemnatory, many saw sense in his views and Henry himself eventually followed Luther's ideology and broke away from Rome, although his motives were undoubtedly more secular than Luther would have wished.

Interestingly, Luther held some merciless anti-Semitic views and was highly antagonistic towards the Jews. Although all Lutheran denominations later condemned this aspect of Luther's teachings, he undoubtedly played a significant part in the growth of anti-Semitism in Europe.

8. THE BURNINGS CONTINUE

By the end of 1557 the queen was looking old and frail. Her health was poor and it showed in the lines and creases across her face. Never a big woman she appeared to have shrunk and was clearly depressed. It seemed that everyone knew about her menstrual problems and that alone was enough to infuriate any woman, let alone the queen of England. Disappointment—in religion, in politics and in her private life—had hit her hard: 'She loved her husband, but he obviously cared little for her. She loved her people, but they remained stubbornly addicted to religious attitudes which to her were sinful.'[1]

She must have known, instinctively, that her end was not that far away and by dying childless, Mary also knew that her sister Elizabeth would succeed her. Elizabeth had been involved, indirectly, in a number of Protestant plots, in name if not in deed. While she made great show of 'playing the game' with Mary there was no doubting her preference to remain apart from Rome. Her succession to the throne would inevitably mean another schism, another break from the church that Mary loved so much. Yet there was nothing that she could do. Small wonder, then, that Mary seemed to be carrying the woes of the world on her shoulders.

The one thing Mary could do was to continue the work of cleansing the country of heretics. To stop the burnings would be to admit defeat; to continue would at least show the Pope that she was no heretic and that her whole regime—including Cardinal Pole—was committed to the Catholic Church. In the final months of Mary's life, nothing would change. Those heretics who were brought to judgement before Bonner and his fellow bishops showed no sign of changing, either. They were as committed to their faith as Mary was to hers.

The tragedy was that neither side could understand the other. No amount of burnings would ever sway the committed Protestants and quite apart from the religious aspects of the divide, while the Spanish influence remained strong at court, English Protestants would never accept the strictures of Catholicism.

Although Mary could not see it—or, at the very least, was not prepared to see it—Protestantism had become a symbol, not of faith but of unstinting opposition to Spain and all her powers. In England hatred of the Spanish had become hugely significant, to the extent that Philip was blamed for much of the persecution. It was not true, of course, and he had on several occasions advised Mary to rein in her eagerness to rid the country of heretics.

¶ The burning of fixe Martyrs at Caunterbury.

Martyrs go to the stake.

Mary would have none of it. She was determined to cleanse the country, regardless of the cost. That was her God-given mission, the reason she had been put on earth.

On 31 January 1556 five martyrs were burned together at Canterbury, all at the same time. Four of them were women: Agnes Snoth, Anne Wright, Joan Sole and Joan Catmer. The sole male was John Lomas, a young man from Tenterden. The spectacle of four women being executed at the same time was what made this burning different, as the crowds who turned up to watch readily agreed. As John Foxe wrote: 'Seldom in any country, for political controversy, have four women been led to execution, whose lives were irreproachable and whom the pity of savages would have spared.'[2] All five were burned in one fire but because of their number two stakes were needed. They died, apparently, singing hymns and psalms.

As the executions continued there was a growing tendency to move away from individual burnings at various locations, some of them at very small and insignificant towns like Horndon-on-the-Hill and Stenning. Instead, authorities moved to a process of group executions at more important or significant centres, places such as Canterbury, Winchester and the capital, London.

Rationalized at the time as a necessary move because of Protestant opposition, even John Foxe felt inclined to repeat the explanation. However, it is hard not to see this change as anything more than a public relations exercise that would enable more people being gathered together to watch the proceedings. The movement of condemned heretics to one or two central spots would also ease the logistical problem of transporting prisoners on an ad hoc basis, a process that was very demanding for the sheriffs and not the safest of practices either.

Now, under the new system, prisoners would have to wait until a sufficient number of heretics had been gathered together in the gaol or courthouse and then, with a full and well-armed guard, the journey could be made. It would stop problems like the one encountered by the sheriff taking Dr Rowland Taylor to Hadleigh for execution: the sheriff and his prisoner had reached Brentwood when a former parishioner came up to Taylor, shook his hand and began a conversation with him. The sheriff immediately pushed the parishioner away and covered Taylor's head with a hood. The condemned man was forced to wear the hood for the rest of his journey to the place of execution.

The Reverend Taylor, hooded after he was recognized and spoken to by a member of the watching crowd as he was taken to the place of execution. The unfortunate Taylor was forced to wear the hood for several miles.

Left: The Martyrs Monument in Canterbury.

Below: Smithfield, the famous meat market in London, became the most infamous of all the execution sites in England.

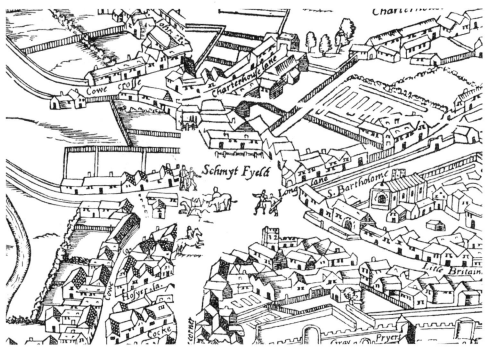

So effective was the reduction of execution sites that by 1558 only thirteen were used. Compared to forty-one in 1555, it was a considerable drop even allowing for the reduced number of burnings in 1558.

Canterbury, with its historical connections to the church along with its cathedral and archbishopric, was an obvious location for executions. In total forty-one people were burned at Martyrs' Field in the city between August 1555 and the summer of 1557. Colchester in Essex became another popular execution centre as did Maidstone and Lewes. Smithfield in London was the scene of many burnings, over forty-men and women perishing there. Of these, seven were the Islington martyrs, burned in June 1558. Six more heretics from Islington were burned that same month at Brentford.

Inevitably, the persecutions, like all witch hunts, gave rise to a number of false accusations as people took advantage of the system and the prevailing attitude of fear to achieve their own agendas.

Catherine Cowchen and her two daughters Perrotine Massey and Guellemine Gilbert lived together on the island of Guernsey where Massey had previously accused a woman by the name of Gosset of stealing a golden goblet.

In revenge, Gosset denounced Massey, her mother and sister, as heretics. All three were found guilty and condemned to the fire but as the flames leaped toward its victims, Perrotine Massey suddenly and surprisingly gave birth to a son. She had not told the authorities that she was pregnant. It might have saved her, delaying her execution at least for a while, but for some reason Massey kept the information to herself.

Now, as the crowd watched in horror, the baby fell from her body into the flames. One of the spectators grabbed the child and pulled it clear. The authorities would have

The three Guernsey women, Katherine Cowchen and her daughters Perrotine Massey and Guillermine Gilbert, who were executed in 1558.

As the flames reach her body, Perrotine Massey gives birth to a baby boy, as this gruesome illustration shows. The baby, like his mother, was immediately condemned to the flames.

none of it and the baby was thrown back into the fire where he, his mother, grandmother and aunt also burned. The horror of the incident supersedes most other examples of man's inhumanity to man during this particularly brutal period of history.[3]

As the burnings continued apace, it sometimes seemed as if new levels of degradation and inhumanity had been reached. Hugh Laverick from Barking was a disabled painter who was able to walk only with the aid of a crutch. John Aprice was blind from birth. Both men appeared before Edmund Bonner on 9 May 1556 accused of heresy. They refused to recant but if they or anyone else thought that their disabilities would ease the bishop's heart or help them in any way they were gravely mistaken. Held at Newgate until the morning of 15 May, Laverick and Aprice were then pushed into a cart and taken to Stratford-le-Bow where they were chained to a stake and burned. As the flames began to lick at his body, Laverick made the only gesture left available to him: he hurled his crutch into the fire, knowing that it was no longer any use to him. He then spoke to Aprice: 'Be of good cheer my brother; for my Lord of London is our good physician; he will heal us both shortly—thee of thy blindness, and me of my lameness.'[4]

Another blind victim, Joan Waste of Derby was executed on 1 August 1556. She had been blind from birth and although she lacked sight she did not lack either belief or courage. At her hearing the inquisitors tried hard to confuse Joan with dogma. The girl held her own but finally, she offered to yield to the doctrine of Bishop Blaine as long as he undertook to answer for her on the Day of Judgement. Her words were at first accepted, then dismissed and Joan declared that she would answer no more questions from such unGodly people.

At the place of execution, Windmill Pit outside Derby, Joan Waste held her brother by the hand, waiting without tears or emotion until the fire was lit and she was dragged away and tied to the stake. As she died she called on the crowd of spectators to pray with her, many of whom complied.

Victims of the burnings increasingly began to use the stake as a pulpit or a platform from which they would make a final statement about their beliefs to the crowd. One constant theme of these statements was the Mass, virtually all of the heretics denying that the body and blood of Christ were present in the bread and wine. The Pope also came in for harsh criticism from the condemned.

It was hard to silence the prisoners who retained the rapt attention of the crowd. Attempts were made, however, as in the case of John Denley, executed on 8 August 1555: 'While suffering in agony, and singing a psalm, Dr Story inhumanely ordered one of the tormentors to throw a faggot at him [Denley], which cut his face, caused him to cease singing, and to raise his hands to his face. Just as Dr Story was remarking in jest that he had spoiled a good song, the pious martyr again chanted, spread his hands abroad in the flames and through Christ Jesus resigned his soul into the hands of his Maker.'[5]

It was not long before the process of execution had become almost a symbolic act, a way that adherents of the true religion—in this case Protestantism—could express their faith, by word, action and by deed.

The execution site, Windmill Hill Pit, for blind Joan Waste.

Many of the martyrs wore long white shirts, made specifically for the occasion of their execution. There was a purpose to the garments: the shirts were an allusion to the white-coated martyrs from the Book of Revelation. According to the Book, all of the martyrs would return to the world on the Day of Judgement for justification and vengeance. The practical side of such clothing was that thick woollen shirts, trousers and skirts were hardier and took longer to burn and therefore made the pain that much more difficult to bear.[6]

Fewer heretics were burned in 1558 than in any other year of Mary's reign. The previous year had seen the burnings peak at around eighty. Exact figures are hard to ascertain with some dates being unrecorded or left blank but it is known that in June 1557 alone twenty-eight went to the stake. There were many reasons for the decline. To begin with there were simply not the numbers of Protestants around, at least not intransigent or determined ones. The burnings had either killed them off or forced them to flee. Either way it meant that the numbers were no longer there.

A devastating outbreak of influenza hit the country in late 1557 and returned again early the following year. Epidemics such as this knew no class barriers and hundreds of officials, from sheriffs to magistrates, perished in the outbreak. Even the queen herself contracted the influenza and was laid low for a short period.

Perhaps the upper classes did not have quite the same natural immunity that so many members of the lower classes, the peasants and subsistence farmers who lived in hovels and ate scraps, had built up over the course of their lives. There are no records of the number of men and women from the lower classes who died during the outbreaks. Whether they died or were just out of action for a few months, the epidemic meant a drastic reduction in the number of officials able to oversee the arrests, confessions and burnings. It was inevitable, therefore, that the process slowed.

By the second half of the year it was also clear Mary was dying. Within the establishment the desire to burn Protestants had largely gone; the practical side of human nature said that sooner or later Elizabeth would succeed her sister and with the queen-in-waiting being of decidedly Protestant leanings it was felt that it was better not to be too ardent in the matter of executions. It did not stop the burnings completely and for the unlucky ones the terror of the fire was omnipresent.

One martyr to go to the stake in 1558 was Richard Sharpe, a weaver from Bristol. Originally brought before the Chancellor of Bristol in 1556, he chose to recant but then had second thoughts: 'He came into the parish church and after high Mass, stood in the church door and said, in a loud voice "Neighbours, bear me record that yonder idol," pointing to the altar, "is the greatest and most abominable that ever was; and I am sorry that I ever denied my Lord God!" At night he was apprehended and carried

Five martyrs go to
the flames.

to Newgate.'[7] He was held in prison for some time but on 7 May 1558 he was burned. Thomas Hale, a shoemaker, also from Bristol, was executed at the same time. He and Sharpe were bound back to back and died confessing the Protestant Articles of Faith.

The last five martyrs burned during the reign of Mary went to the stake just six days before she died. They were Alice Snoth, Catherine Wright, John Corneford, C. Browne and John Herst, all of them from Kent. According to Foxe, their executions might have been delayed but 'The archdeacon of Canterbury, judging that the sudden death of the queen would suspend execution, travelled post back from London to have the satisfaction of adding another page to the black list of papistical sacrifices.'[8]

One man who nearly escaped the pyre was Thomas Benbridge from Hampshire. Benbridge had consistently denied the sacraments and even went so far as to state that the Devil was actually the head of the Catholic Church. He was sent to the stake in July 1558. The fire was badly built, and burned slowly. As the flames reached his legs Benbridge screamed out that he recanted. The fire was immediately broken down by friends of the victim who then dragged him to safety while Dr Seaton, the priest who had been present to give the death sermon, hastily scribbled out some words of recantation for Benbridge to sign: 'He signed on the spot, using the back of a stooped bystander as a writing desk. The sheriff, Sir Richard Pecksall, the Marquis of Winchester's son-in-law, called the execution off on his own authority.'[9] The Privy Council was not best pleased, believing the recantation was pretence and the sheriff was ordered to have Benbridge executed directly, regardless of the previous recantation. This was done, Benbridge being put to death on another badly built fire which John Foxe reported 'did rather broyle him, than burn him'.[10]

The Marian burnings were the work of a religious fanatic who managed, on the whole, to take the country with her into a wild and terrifying period of madness. The tragedy of the whole affair is that Mary genuinely believed she was right, that she was doing the work God wanted her to do. In that there are undoubtedly modern equivalents.

Hampton Court reenactors 'Anne Boleyn' and her venal cousin 'Sir Francis Bryan' capture perfectly the dress codes of the time. Anne, of course, suffered Tudor wrath and was beheaded, in what was a particularly messy affair. (Duncan Harris)

9. HERETIC HUNTERS

If there were going to be heretics—and the Catholic Church said that there were—it stood to reason that there would have to be heretic hunters to hunt them down. In many instances Bloody Mary's heresy hunters were the bishops of the various dioceses, men who had a vested interest in raking around and exposing anyone who did not conform to Catholic principles. These men were usually assisted by zealous assistants, some lay men, some from the church.

Bishop Bonner in London, the most assiduous of the hunters, was helped by the Harpsfield brothers, John and Nicholas, and commissaries like John Kingston. Both of the Harpsfields were clergymen and both efficient and hardworking heresy hunters. Nicholas Harpsfield was so committed to the business of cleansing the country of Protestants that as archdeacon he also headed up Pole's team at Canterbury.

Other heresy-hunting bishops included John Hopton of Norwich, Ralph Baynes at Lichfield and, at Chichester, Bishop John Christopherson. These powerful men ruled like kings in their dioceses, sniffing out even the slightest hint of heresy. Cardinal Pole had introduced a system of legatine visitations for all of the dioceses in the country, to run from April 1556. The discovery of heresy, wherever it might be lurking, was the major task of the visitations

Unlike the later witch finders of Salem and seventeenth-century Europe, the Marian heresy hunters laid heavy emphasis on observation. Sixteenth-century England was still a largely illiterate society and, as a rule, people did not refine their religious views by reading banned books or illegal tracts and pamphlets. Naturally, there were some who went this way and for those the sudden search, at night or other times when a visit was least expected, did reveal a modicum of illicit literature. For most of the time, however, it was a case of the heresy hunters observing, listening and watching for what people said or did. That meant appearing in churches on a regular basis, talking to other worshippers and, most effective of all, watching what these worshippers did. Perhaps more importantly they watched what people did not do.

The heresy hunters were instructed to ensure that worshippers made full use of the facilities at church as failing to comply with even one aspect of the service could well signify the presence of a heretic. It meant that they had, among other things, to observe devout use of elements such as holy water and keep a keen lookout for inappropriate behaviour during Mass. Worshippers who lurked behind pillars or averted their gaze when the Host was elevated were immediately suspect. Attendance at church service was monitored and always there was the terror of insistent questioning: 'Why have you not been to church these past six weeks?'[1]

Questioning was always feared and the hunters were not above browbeating their victims or asking leading questions. When all else failed, there was always violence. The vicar of Aylesbury, a man by the name of Berry, was renowned for his evil temper and his propensity to use his fists: 'He struck a poor man for a trifling word, with a flail, which proved fatal for the offending object. He also gave a woman named Alice Oxes so heavy a blow with his fist, as she met him when entering the hall when he was in an ill-humour that she died.'[2] Such behaviour was rare. Normally the heresy hunters were a little more subtle in their approach to would-be heretics.

Nicholas Harpsfield was one of the more active heresy hunters, particularly in the Weald of Kent where Pole, as the new Archbishop of Canterbury, was making his mark. Harpsfield marauded across the region looking, particularly, for ordinary lay men and women—there were others who could take care of the clergy. By the end of May 1556 he had apparently arrested fifteen lay heretics. Ten more were arrested and executed by January 1557 and another fourteen by the summer.[3] What he was searching for were people who had failed to take communion recently, who absented themselves from church or refused holy bread and water. Men who were known in their local communities as possessing good voices and had sung in church during the reign of Edward were now required to join the parish choir for Mass and other important ceremonies and Nicholas Harpsfield was there to make sure they conformed.

Harpsfield was not alone in attempting to eradicate every heretic on earth. Sir John Baker of Cranfield was so ardent that he even opened up his own gaol. It was situated above the porch of the parish church where incarcerated Protestants would be able to hear the Catholic services and the hymns that went on just a few yards from their heads. Bishop Bonner imprisoned heretics in his coal house while they were waiting for transportation to gaol. Lighting the coal might have been one way of keeping warm but, of course, the prisoners had no means of setting a fire.

Kent, East Anglia and Essex were something of a Protestant enclave, possibly due to their closeness to the Continent and, of course, to London which saw thousands of travellers arriving and departing every day. The port of London regularly brought in heretical books; it also saw the arrival and departure of dozens of Protestant evangelists. And, if necessary, the Norfolk or Suffolk coastlines were good places to take ship and escape.

In 1555 commissions against heresy were set up in these regions to oversee and consolidate the heresy-hunting activities of magistrates and other officials. It was probably a necessary bureaucratic move but the connotations of dictatorship, even comparison to the later rule of Cromwell's major generals, cannot be avoided.

Meeting regularly, the commissions would pass on the names and sometimes even the bodies of suspected heretics to the bishops. That was when their fate would be decided. It was a system of sorts, a fairly basic system but still a system, an attempt to control the ad hoc nature of heresy hunting that had marked the earlier stages of the Marian persecutions.

The commissions sometimes relied on informants, either groups or individuals who had information likely to condemn unsuspecting members of the community. One example is the group that compiled the Ipswich Dossier, a file of information on possible Protestants in the area. Such information was invaluable to the commissioners.

Sometimes the informants went a stage further. Matthew Butler and Dr Richard Argentine, both members of the group that had compiled the Ipswich Dossier, led a squad of would-be heresy hunters to track down the fugitive Agnes Wardell who, they were reliably informed, had made a fleeting visit to her Ipswich home. Their raid was a failure, however, as Agnes escaped by hiding in a cupboard and then in a nettle-filled ditch before friendly townspeople distracted the searchers and helped her to safety.[4]

The Reverend Thomas Tye of Much Bentley had originally been a Protestant preacher, a gospeller, during the reign of Edward VI and when Mary came to the throne had spent twelve months hiding in the woods and dilapidated barns of his former parish. Within the year, however, he underwent a complete change of heart, converted to Catholicism and with his background of evangelical Protestantism became one of the most effective heresy hunters in the eastern shires; after all, he knew the opposition and how they thought. His forte was the night raid when he and his assistants would swoop on sleeping and unsuspecting Protestants. Furious at Bishop Bonner's decision not to prosecute a group of twenty-two heretics, the Essex Twenty-Two as they were known, Tye conducted his own campaign against individual members of the group.

Bonner's decision not to proceed against the Essex Twenty-two—on the advice of Cardinal Pole—was taken because by 1557 the execution of such a large group, all from the same area and all known to each other, would be counterproductive for Mary's regime. Individuals were a different matter, Tye decided.

On 7 March 1557 Tye led a typical night raid on the house of William Munt. Along with his wife Alice and daughter Rose Allin, Munt had been one of the Essex Twenty-Two and on their release from custody refused to attend church. Munt and his family not only refused to attend themselves but, tempting fate, they actually chastised those who did. It was inevitable that Bonner would not stand the insult for long. On the night of the raid Munt and his wife were in bed, Alice being ill, but Tye and

Left: Tye and Tyrell, heretic hunters, at work during a night raid.

Below: Rose Allin is held and tortured by Edmund Tyrell after a raid on her parents' house. Burned on the hand, she defied Tyrell but was later burned at the stake.

The burning of Rose Allins hand, by Edmund Tyrrell, as she was going to fetch drinke for her Mother, lying ſicke in her bedde.

one of his officers encountered Rose Allin in the passageway, taking her mother a drink. Tye's companion immediately went into action: 'Seizing the young woman by the wrist, he held the lighted candle under her hand, burning it crosswise on the back, until the tendons divided from the flesh, during which he loaded her with many opprobrious epithets. She endured his rage unmoved.'⁵

William and Alice Munt, their daughter Rose and seven others from the original Essex Twenty-Two were arrested and burned at Colchester on 2 August 1557.

Perhaps two of the most famous of the heresy hunters were Sir John and Edmund Tyrrell from Essex. They were related to the Nicholas Tyrrell who, as custodian of the Tower of London, probably had a more than fleeting involvement with the disappearance of the two princes in the Tower during the reign of Richard III. That summed up the family: self-interested and desperate for anything that would advance their social standing in the county.

Both Tyrrells were brutal and unrelenting in their pursuit of heretics and would go to almost any length to achieve a confession. Edmund was the man who tortured Rose Allin by burning her hand during the midnight raid on the Munt house. Like Tye, both of the Tyrrell's were advocates of the midnight raid, believing that the terror induced by smashing in the front door of a house while the occupants were sleeping was the least that heretics deserved. For a brief period they had enormous power, interrogating suspects at their own country houses, quite probably using torture and violence to extract confessions.

And then there was Justice 'Nine Holes' Drayner. A magistrate from Smarden in Kent, he was accorded the epithet 'Nine Holes' for a very specific reason: 'Drayner made in the rood loft nine holes, that he might look about the Church at Mass time ... He would stand to see who looked not or held not up his hands thereto: which person not doing, he would trouble and punish very sore.'⁶ Aided and abetted by his minister and other officers of the local church, Drayner undoubtedly caught out many people, guilty and innocent alike, by this ploy. One glance away from the altar, one stifled yawn behind a shielding hand and Drayner would pounce. The nine separate holes enabled him to see almost every corner of the church and no-one could escape his eagle eye.

It would not be putting too fine a point on the subject to say that the heresy hunters established a reign of terror, particularly in the eastern counties of England. They, like Mary, were driven by the desire to do God's work. There were others, however, who undoubtedly had more prosaic motives, even if it was just the desire to flex their muscles and display the powers they had been suddenly given.

By 1557 Mary, like many of the myrmidons who did her work, cannot have failed to see that the people, her subjects, were already looking to the future. In particular,

The Martyrs' Tree outside Brentwood School in Essex was the place of execution for William Hunter, a young apprentice.

Mary's half-sister, Elizabeth, pictured here as queen, ruled for forty-four glorious years in what became England's golden age.

Mary, pictured here on a Victorian 'reward' or 'merit' card, looking young, beautiful and fresh-faced. At one time she indeed boasted all these attributes.

they were looking to Elizabeth as her successor. It may have been unpalatable but in the event of Mary having no heir—and it was increasingly looking as if this would be the case—there was only her half-sister Elizabeth. Despite this fairly obvious resolution to the problem of succession, the heresy hunters continued with their work, almost to the end. They had set their course and were intent on following their star wherever it might lead.

10. DIGNITY TO THE LAST

In July 1557 Mary once again began to believe that she was pregnant. The dates fitted—just—and eventually she wrote to her husband to tell him the good news. A child, a Catholic child, would make everything all right, would confirm that the reign of terror she had instigated had been correct and that her work was now about to be blessed by God.

Philip was delighted. The news, he said, had almost made up for the loss of Calais. Nevertheless, he realized that Mary had waited until the sixth month of her supposed pregnancy before telling him about the baby—a little unusual, perhaps? And so he sent the Count of Feria to England to verify the story.

What Feria discovered was that, unlike the previous time Mary had claimed to be pregnant, no arrangements had been made for the queen's confinement and she had not moved to Hampton Court, which would have been the usual practice. And

Queen Mary: already she knows that the burnings have been in vain and that when she becomes queen, Elizabeth will undo all of the reforms recently introduced.

yet she certainly looked pregnant. Her belly was swollen, and her talk was all about the coming child.

Listening to her, spending time in her company, Feria concluded that, despite appearances, Mary was deceiving herself once again. The queen, however, was convinced that this time it was the real thing.

At the end of March Mary rewrote her will, a customary precaution for any woman of substance approaching the ninth month of her confinement. The crown would be left to her heir, even though no such person yet existed, apart from her half-sister Elizabeth. Princess Elizabeth was not named, deliberately, as Mary still hoped for a child of her own. If she was to die before such a child came of age then her husband Philip would act as regent.

Mary's ninth month came and passed, and the tenth. Clearly she was not pregnant as she was now forced to admit. This time, however, it was more than simply a phantom pregnancy, wish fulfilment at its extreme; this time it was not just a psychological problem; this time there was physical illness as well.

Whatever had caused the swelling to her belly was tight, firm and still there, her doctors told her. It was certainly not wind, as many of the detractors of her previous pregnancy had believed then and believed now. It was in fact a growth, a massive growth; doctors could feel it and ponder what it might be although medical opinion of the time had no understanding of what ailed her.

The queen's health had deteriorated sharply in the past few months although right to the end none of her doctors could say what exactly was wrong with her. She could not sleep and sometimes her eyesight failed her. She suffered from severe headaches and fevers that lanced into her withered body and confined her to her bed.[1]

In August Mary, her resistance already at nought, caught influenza, a virulent strain that was again raging across the country. Moved to St James's Palace, she was finally forced to publicly admit that she was not pregnant and would be never. In a codicil to her will she stated that on her death she would be succeeded by the next

The remains of a martyr, carried away at night.

in line to the throne. She still did not actually name Elizabeth but it was clear whom she meant. She had grown progressively weaker but only now, many years later, it seems fairly clear that she was suffering from ovarian or cervical cancer.[2] That would explain the growth in her stomach.

While Philip strove to endear himself with Elizabeth, the Count of Feria being dispatched to pay court and even arrange a marriage for her to a suitable Catholic prince. Elizabeth was grateful for Philip's concerns but she had no intention of marrying anyone at the moment, certainly not the Duke of Savoy as Feria was suggesting.

Mary, meanwhile, was fighting for her life and in early November her condition seemed to improve a little. Despite this she was constantly being urged to be more specific about her successor. Finally, after much soul-searching, she agreed and named Elizabeth as the next monarch.

It was a heart-breaking decision for Mary. She had spent most of her time as queen trying to avoid such an announcement but now she simply had no choice. Delegates from the Privy Council were dispatched to Hatfield House to inform the princess. Mary's final communication to Elizabeth urged her to keep the Catholic religion as it had been re-established in England. Even as she made the request Mary knew that it was a forlorn hope.

Her condition now spiralled rapidly downward. For the last few days of her life much of her time was spent in a coma. When, every so often, she emerged from this trance-like state she told her ladies-in-waiting that she had experienced lovely dreams with dozens of children playing music and singing wonderful songs to her. Just before midnight on 16 November 1588, with the end clearly in sight, she received the last rites. At some time between five and six the following morning, 17 November, she died in great pain, both physical and emotional.

Elizabeth was formally proclaimed Queen just six hours after her sister's death. The city of London marked her accession by the ringing of church bells and the lighting of bonfires.

Philip—whose rank and status as king within England expired on the death of his wife—expressed regret at Mary's passing but, in all honestly, he was more upset by the death of his father, Charles V, who had died only a few weeks before. In his letter to Feria he ordered the count to represent him with dignity at the queen's funeral—and to make sure he took possession of the jewels that Mary had bequeathed him in her will.

By a strange quirk of fate Cardinal Pole died just twelve hours after Mary. There was symmetry in the two deaths, as Pole himself noted from his deathbed. It was as if he could not bear to carry on once the lynchpin of his world, his mission, had gone. He died still not reconciled to the Pope and, like Mary, knowing his work was unfinished.

At the end Mary died in confusion, disappointment and dissatisfaction. Her love for her people, her subjects, had never diminished but she had never been able to accept religious practices that she found abhorrent and heretical. She loved her husband but distance and time had taken their toll. Philip was fond of her but no more. She loved the Catholic Church and yet, at the end of her life, she was in serious conflict with the Pope. Her love for God had not changed but, for some unfathomable reason, he had chosen not to bless her with a child. With Elizabeth as her successor, it would mean an undoing of all that she had begun. At the end Mary must have known that the burnings had been counterproductive. They might have forced Protestantism underground but they had certainly not destroyed it. Arguably, with the coming of Elizabeth the Catholic faith in England was about to nose-dive into a black hole from which there would be little or no chance of rescue.

Mary's funeral took place on 14 December, her body having lain in state for three weeks. She was buried in Westminster Abbey, in a tomb where many years later she would be joined by her sister. The funeral oration was given by John White, now Bishop of Winchester, the man who had replaced Stephen Gardiner after his death. He repaid his debt to Mary with a sermon that praised the dead queen but was less than welcoming of the new queen, Elizabeth.

The following day White was placed under house arrest and before the year was out fourteen of Mary's bishops had been deprived of their bishoprics and also placed under house arrest. All of them had refused to take Elizabeth's Oath of Supremacy.

As might have been expected, only one bishop—Anthony Kitchin of Llandaff—took the oath and was restored to his bishopric. That made it four monarchs of vastly differing religious convictions that the self-interested and vacillating Kitchin had served.

As far as the clergy was concerned, 137 either resigned or were deprived of their livings by Elizabeth, leaving 124 in post. Out of the seventy-seven cathedral dignitaries, forty-three were deprived or resigned. All in all it meant that over half of Mary's dignitaries—archdeacons, deans and the like—were not prepared to serve the new queen.[3] This was not necessarily a bad thing for Elizabeth: she could now build her church the way she wanted without having to deal with too many of the die-hard Catholics that Mary had put in post.

The burnings continued right to the end of Mary's life. She died in mid-November but had clearly been ill for some time before that. It did not bring her a sudden rush of magnanimity. No fewer than elven martyrs died that November, two of them—John Herst and Kathleen Knight—on the 15th, going to the fires just two days before Mary's death.[4]

Cardinal Pole was equally as committed as his queen, convinced that the way they had chosen was the only way. While he always preferred recantation, Pole still

The queen in waiting, Henry's second daughter, Elizabeth.

believed that for those intractable members of the Protestant faith there was only one solution—the fire.

Mary's two great compatriots, Gardiner and Pole, died with her. Of the others, little is known but very few lived out long and comfortable lives.

Bishop Bonner—who, incidentally, was known as Bloody Bonner long before his queen became Bloody Mary—was ordered to resign his bishopric when Elizabeth came to the throne. Amazingly, he refused point blank. Quite what he hoped to achieve is unknown but, then, he was always something of a law unto himself.

It was inevitable that Elizabeth would not allow such a situation to last for long and in April 1560 Bonner ended up in the Marshalsea Prison. According to some reports he lived a comfortable life—as all prisoners could if they had the money to pay for little luxuries.

Despite numerous attempts to have him executed, Bonner seemed to bear a charmed life. Elizabeth simply let him sweat. He survived until 5 September 1569 when he died in prison of natural causes.

Dr Story, who had once encouraged his constables to hurl faggots at a burning heretic, was imprisoned but escaped to the Continent where he lived for some years. At one stage he managed to obtain a commission from the Duke of Alba to search all the ships docking at Antwerp, looking for heretical books. Story had not been forgotten, however. Kidnapped and taken immediately to England, he was condemned

The final image: Maidstone martyrs dying for their faith in the flames of Mary's bonfires.

and locked up in prison. After some considerable time he was transported to Tyburn where he was hanged, drawn and quartered.

John and Nicholas Harpsfield, two of the most efficient heresy hunters of Mary's reign, both found themselves incarcerated in the Fleet Prison. Due to poor health, Nicholas was released from captivity and died in 1576.

So ended the Marian persecutions; a killing spree that originated from, and was driven by, Queen Mary. It was a purge that almost rivalled the cynical and cold-blooded murders of Vlad the Impaler in Romania.

So great were the numbers killed between 1555 and 1558 that sometimes we forget the good things that emerged from Mary's reign. And there were a few: 'She restored the Navy, renewed the coinage and increased crown revenue. She also established new hospitals, improved the education of the clergy and increased the authority of local government.'[5] The most important of these was the changes she made to the revenue of the country.

Duties on trade were increased and improved, customs revenues rose from £25,000 in 1553 to over £80,000 per annum at the end of Mary's reign. It was something which greatly aided Elizabeth in her wars and general policies in the years to come.[6]

The terrible change in character of Mary Tudor, from a mischievous, high-spirited young girl to a thoughtful and repressed teenager to a murderous, cold-hearted tyrant is a study in how one individual and the events of that life can have such a profound effect on a whole nation.

If there is one word to sum up the queen it has to be loneliness. Deprived of her mother's love and guidance, starved of understanding and compassion from her father, her treatment was bound to have a detrimental effect. Long years of living under close house arrest and in fear of death would not have helped. Finally joined in marriage to Philip of Spain, to be cast off and ignored, as her mother before her had been, was the last straw.

The real sadness of Mary was simply that Catholicism, once rejected by the people of England, was never going to come back as the sole religion of the country. The American historian Garrett Mattingly probably summed it up best: 'For such Londoners as had cheerfully gone to Mass in old Queen Mary's time, choking down whatever disgust they felt at the reek of the fires in Smithfield, even to such as would

Marshalsea Prison.

go again without obvious reluctance if that were the best way to secure their business and their families ... the continued life of the Catholic party presented a dreadful menace.'[7] Mary was undoubtedly devout; the vast majority of her people were not. The 'dreadful menace' that Mattingly wrote about was not just a theological problem. It was real, it was tactile and tangible, it was ever-present and it was the potential for persecution and for war.

Ultimately, Mary set herself up as a martyr, not deliberately or even consciously. But in her unswerving dedication to her cause, in her determination to battle on alone and in effectively working and worrying herself into an early grave, martyrdom was exactly what she achieved.

Most of those about to face the execution fires refused to recant; Mary, in her own way, also refused to recant, to go back on her beliefs. She refused to back down even when she knew that her cause was doomed and that her sister would soon undo everything that the Marian Reformation had achieved. And she did it uncomplainingly. She misjudged what her God wanted her to do; that did not, necessarily, make her a bad person—just a sad one.

In happier times: the 1553 entry of Queen Mary I into London, with Princess Elizabeth looking on. By John Byam Liston Shaw (1910), Palace of Westminster Collection (BBC Your Paintings / PD-Art)

Julia Marlowe, the acclaimed Shakespearian actress, as Mary Tudor in Paul Kester's 1904 Broadway adaptation of *When Knighthood was in Flower*, a show that played to packed houses. (Plays of the Present)

CONCLUSION

Only two British monarchs are known predominantly for their cruelty and for the bloodthirsty nature of their times in power, Richard III and Mary Tudor. Others might be renowned for their stupidity (King John and Henry VI), their money-grabbing meanness (Henry VII) or their lack of humour and directness (Victoria). Cruelty was a different matter.

So, the bad monarchs of Britain? There are always saving graces and nothing is quite as simple as it seems at first glance. Richard did what he had to do in order to prevent a return to the chaos of the Wars of the Roses. Mary was driven by her faith and did what she did because, in her mind, that was what God wanted her to do. The actions and reactions of both monarchs have to be taken in the context of the time when they ruled.

Mary inherited her problems. If her father had managed to find one, two or even three male heirs with Catherine of Aragon there would have been no divorce, no break with Rome—and, inevitably, no Marian counter-reformation. There would, quite probably, have been no Queen Mary. The whole course of British history would have been different.

Mary did the best she could, wrongly it must be admitted and with tragic results. She had been dealt a poor hand and because of her character deficiencies, did not see any reasonable way of rectifying or improving that hand. Unreasonable ways, on the other side of the coin, were plentiful and obvious—enter the burnings.

The ramifications of her persecutions were and continue to be vast. The only other Catholic monarch of Britain after Mary was driven from his throne in 1688 and even now Catholics remain very much on the fringe of society. No English monarch has, since Mary's time, ever married a Catholic.

Even before Mary died there was a sense of excitement in the air and a belief that now, after five years of Hell, things would be different. Already the old queen was being vilified: 'It was a Thursday, and they called the day before, when rumour spread that Mary Tudor was dying, Hope Wednesday. As its first and later anniversaries came round, many minds must have recalled the event and hearts warmed in devout thankfulness.'[1]

In Ireland and Scotland the differences between Catholics and Protestants still sometimes flare up in conflict or, in the case of Northern Ireland, into actual warfare. Much of this has to be attributed to the horror of Mary's burnings. No amount of argument or justification can ever absolve Mary Tudor from the horror of her reign. She knew what she was doing and if there ever was the tiniest sliver of doubt, she pushed it away and got on with the job. She got it wrong. In the circumstances, given the era and the people around her, it is difficult to know if she could have done anything different. That dilemma remains a part of Mary's tragedy.

The Green Dragon Inn, Wymondham, **Norfolk**

Notes

Two versions of *Foxe's Book of Martyrs* have been used: the full, unabridged version which is available online, with commentary, at British Academy Actes and Monuments; and the abridged version, originally published in 1589, several versions of which are available and most of them with excellent introductions.

Introduction

1. Thomas Penn, *The Winter King*, Penguin, pp. 377-8.
2. Roger Lockyer, *Tudor and Stuart Britain*, Longmans, p. 123.
3. William Byron Forbrush, foreword in *Foxe's Book of Martyrs*, Hendrickson Publishers, p. XI.

1. A Birth is Announced

1. Anna Whitelock, *Mary Tudor: England's First Queen*, Bloomsbury, p. 18.
2. https://en.wikipedia.org/wiki/Mary_1_of_England
3. Ibid.
4. Penn, pp. 70-1.
5. Whitelock, p. 58.

2. The Lady Mary

1. Calendar of State Papers (Spanish) quoted in Whitelock, p. 88.
2. Lockyer, p. 99.
3. Whitelock, *Mary Tudor*, p. 13.
4. Quoted in Elizabeth Norton *The Lives of Tudor Women*, p. 54.
5. British Academy Foxe Project, *Actes and Monuments*, Book 7.

3. Queen at Last

1. Whitelock, Mary Tudor, p.180.
2. J. E. Neale, *Queen Elizabeth I*, p. 34.
3. Eamon Duffy, *Fires of Faith*, Yale, p. 4.
4. Ibid, pp. 4-5.
5. Anna Whitelock, 'Mary: Queen Against the Odds' in 'Royal Women' in *BBC History* magazine, 2017.
6. H. A. L. Fisher, *A History of Europe*, Fontana, Page 517
7. Duffy, p. 11.
8. Ibid, p. 12.

4. The Spanish Match

1. John Foxe, *Foxe's Book of Martyrs*, abridged version, p. 264.
2. Quoted in Lockyer, p. 1.
3. www.luminarium.org/enclopedia/queenmary/htm

4. R. Trevor Davies, *The Golden Century of Spain*, MacMillan, pp. 108-9.
5. Lockyer, p. 124.
6. British Academy Foxe Project, Book 10, pp. 1418-9.
7. Whitelock, *Mary* Tudor, p. 216.
8. Lockyer, p. 125.
9. Simon Schama, *A History of Britain*, BBC, p. 325.
10. Wikipedia, ibid.
11. Schama, p. 325.
12. Lockyer, p. 126.

5. The Burnings Begin

1. Duffy, pp. 58-9.
2. British Academy Foxe Project, Book 7.
3. Foxe, abridged, p. 268.
4. Ibid, p. 275.
5. Schama, p. 325
6. Foxe, abridged, p. 283.
7. Whitelock, *Mary Tudor*, p. 264.
8. British Academy Foxe Project, Book 11, p. 1981.
9. Elizabeth Norton, *The Lives of Tudor Women*, Head of Zeus, p. 254.

6. Even the Archbishop

1. Lockyer, p. 127.
2. Foxe, abridged, p. 299.
3. British Academy Foxe Project, Book 1, p. 1770.
4. Foxe, abridged, p. 172.
5. Duffy, pp. 147-8.
6. Foxe, abridged, p. 310.
7. www.spartacus-educational.com
8. British Academy Foxe Project, Book 11, p. 1887.
9. Ibid, p. 1888.
10. Ibid.
11. Anon, 'The Execution of Archbishop Cranmer' in John Carey *The Faber Book of Reportage*, Faber & Faber.
12. www.wikipedia.org.wiki/Thomas_Cranmer

7. Excommunicate

1. Duffy, p. 116.
2. Whitelock, *Mary Tudor*, p. 278.
3. Lockyer, p. 129.

8. The Burnings Continue

1. Lockyer, p. 131.
2. Foxe, abridged, p. 304.
3. https://en.wikipedia.org/wiki/Mary_1_of_England
4. Whitelock, *Mary Tudor*, p. 265.
5. Foxe, abridged, p. 123.
6. Duffy, p. 169.
7. Foxe, abridged, p. 351.
8. Ibid.
9. Duffy, p. 169.
10. British Academy Foxe Project, Book 12, pp. 2246-7.

9. Heretic Hunters

1. Duffy, p. 131.
2. Foxe, abridged, p. 338.
3. Duffy, p. 132.
4. Ibid, p. 136.
5. Foxe, abridged, p. 328.
6. British Academy Foxe Project, Book 12, Page 2111-2.

10. Dignity to the Last

1. Whitelock, *Mary Tudor*, p. 300.
2. Schama, p. 328.
3. Duffy, p. 197.
4. List of Protestant Martyrs of the English Reformation at https://en.wikipedia.org
5. 'Queen Mary 1st' at www.historyextra.com
6. Lockyer, p. 131.
7. Garrett Mattingly, *The Defeat of the Spanish Armada*, Jonathan Cape, p. 23.

Conclusion

1. J. E. Neale, *The Age of Catherine de Medici*, p. 95.

Bibliography

Primary sources

Foxe, John, *Actes and Monuments*, aka *Foxe's Book of Martyrs*, available online @ British Academy Foxe Project (with commentaries).

————, *Foxe's Book of Martyrs*, Hendrickson Publishers, Massachusetts, 2004, first published 1589.

Books

Carey, John, *The Faber Book of Reportage*, Faber & Faber, London, 1987.

Duffy, Eamon, *Fires of Faith*, Yale University Press, New York & London, 2009

Fisher, H. A. L. *A History of Europe*, Fontana, London, 1961.

Lockyer, Roger, *Tudor and Stuart Britain, 1485–1714*, Longmans, London, 1967.

Mattingly, Garrett, *The Defeat of the Spanish Armada*, Jonathan Cape, London, 1959.

Neale, J. E., *Elizabeth I*, Penguin, London, 1971.

————, *The Age of Catherine de Medici*, Cape, London, 1966.

Norton, Elizabeth, *The Lives of Tudor Women*, Head of Zeus Ltd., London, 2016.

Penn, Thomas, *Winter King*, Penguin, London, 2011.

Schama, Simon, *A History of Britain: At the Edge of the World*, BBC, London, 2000.

Trevor Davies, R., *The Golden Century of Spain*, MacMillan, London, 1937.

Whitelock, Anna, *Mary Tudor: England's First Queen*, Bloomsbury, London, 2010.

Periodicals

BBC History magazine, 2015–17.

Royal Women, ed. Rob Attar, BBC Publications, 2016.

'The Tudors in 50 Moments' (Tracy Borman), BBC Publications, 2016.

World Histories, BBC Publications, 2017.

Blogs

www.bbc.co.uk/blogs/wales (Rawlins White Goes to the Stake)

www.blog.english-heritage.org.uk

www.tudorsdynasty.com

Websites

www.historyextra.com/ (Queen Mary)

www.luminarium.org/enclopedia/

www.spartacus-educational.com

www.wikipedia.org.wiki/Mary_1_of_England

www.wikipedia.org.wiki/Thomas_Cranmer

Acknowledgements

I have to thank my old history teacher, Dewi Ellis Williams, for imbuing me with a love of his subject—and you would have to love it to sit through those interminable Tuesday and Thursday afternoon diatribes rather than chase a ball around the rugby pitch. In particular, he showed me how to appreciate, even to love, the Tudor and Stuart periods. It was Dewi who taught me to look at the reign of Bloody Mary with open eyes rather than the blinkered peerings that dominated historical thinking at the time. So Dewi, wherever you are, thanks.

Thanks also to my father who was the polar opposite of Dewi: magical, inspirational and totally prejudiced. He believed that Henry VII killed the Princes in the Tower, that Elizabeth was really a man and that Mary knew nothing about the burnings that blighted her reign. Impossible to shake from his opinions, he made talking about History fascinating, even when his views were, frankly, 'off the wall' and was generous enough to share his thoughts with an equally as biased teenager most winter evenings.

Phil Carradice is a poet, novelist and historian. He has written over fifty books, the most recent being *The Call-up: A Study of Peacetime Conscription in Britain* and *Napoleon in Defeat and Captivity*. He presents the BBC Wales history programme *The Past Master* and is a regular broadcaster on both TV and radio. A native of Pembroke Dock, he now lives in the Vale of Glamorgan but travels extensively in the course of his work. Educated at Cardiff University and at Cardiff College of Education, Phil is a former head teacher but now lives as a full-time writer and is regarded as one of Wales's best creative writing tutors. He writes extensively for several Pen & Sword military history series including 'Cold War 1945–1991' and 'History of Terror'.

Index